To Sarah,

Very hearty Congratulations for both your efforts and your achievements during the Scholars Week at Pangbourne. I hope that this will be a fond, if chilly memory of one of the exercises of many years to come. Well done.

Andrew Whale

ARRIVAL PRESS

SPLASH

Edited

By

TIM SHARP

First published in Great Britain in 1996 by
ARRIVAL PRESS
1 - 2 Wainman Road, Woodston,
Peterborough, PE2 7BU

All Rights Reserved

Copyright Contributors 1996

HB ISBN 1 85786 450 6
SB ISBN 1 85786 445 X

Foreword

Whilst editing 'Splash' it became apparent to me that we really do enjoy any hobby, sport or pastime to do with water. Whether it's swimming, surfing, skiing or diving we are all happy to take to the waves and enjoy our leisure activities.

The poems contained in this anthology come from people from all walks of life; the professional, the housewife and the child.

After reading this book I think you will be able to relate to your own aquatic pastimes and pleasures.

Tim Sharp
Editor

CONTENTS

Water, Sun, Boat And Skis	S A Hills	1
The Wave	Mark A Hagerty	2
Why Do We Do It?	Judy Crane	3
Water-Ski Buddies	Wendi Turner	4
Ski Fever	O R Ballard	5
In At The Deep End	Kazzie Ingram	5
H2 O My God!	Joyce Barclay	6
Waterways	G W Bailey	6
Windsurfing	Joan Hands	7
Come Follow	Winifred Wardle	8
Deep In A World Of Wonder	Sarah Tahir	8
Swimming With Style	Richard Bright	9
Shark!	Lynda Blagg	10
Water Dangers	Tony Williams	10
Swimming Lessons	Margaret Sanderson	11
Well Did You Ever	Ben Dearnley	12
Parlaiz Anglais	Joyce M Hefti-Whitney	13
My First Ski	Andrew Whale	14
Seaward Bound	Richard Saunders	15
Sea Song	Peter Francis	16
Divers' Paradise	Vicki Billings	16
Sunrise Sailing	P A Robbins	17
Pure Extreme	Craig Alan Hornby	18
The Sea Survives	David Ball	18
Beginner	Helen Mallourides	19
The Dive	Roy Prentice	20
I Can Swim	Sheila E Harvey	21
Underwater	K G Brough	22
Hesitant	Angela Pearson	22
No Pain!	Kathleen Speed	23
I Prefer Puddles	R Medland	24
Dreams	Selina Patel	24
Simon At Six	John Christopher Cole	25

Memories Of The School Gala	Christine Corbett	26
Water Worship	Pete Harrison	26
The Sea Urchins	Peter Littlefield	27
God Bless The RNLI	Boris	28
Hyperactive Bathing	David Gibbons	29
My First Lesson	Anne Livingstone	30
Untitled	P Fisher	30
How Much For A Pair Of Water Wings?	Naomi Cooke	31
Scuba Tour	Margareth	32
Red Sea Blues	John Hollyer	33
A Stroke Of Luck!	Sharon Goldsmith	34
The Water Babies' Swimming Club	Ted Cowan	35
Beautiful Swimmer	Andrew Hearn	36
Wetbob	Ted Herbert	36
Sink Or Swim	Carol Irving	37
A New Costume	Pip	38
Woman In A Dinghy	Pam Joll	39
I Am A Water Baby	Jill Pettitt	40
Wave	H R Burns	41
Water Sport	Susan Hansen	41
Go With The Flow	Mary Todd	42
The Swimming Lesson	Janice Richer	43
Ben And The Sea	Marie Little	44
Pond Life	Rachel Oxtoby	44
Swimming	Reg Morris	45
Unsynchronised Swimming	Rosemarie Varndell	46
Water Sports	Janet Elizabeth Isherwood	47
Rapid Descent	Andrew Livingstone	47
The Reluctant Swimmer	Genevieve Stone	48
A Verse To Surfing	Eileen-a-Lanna	48
Sailing Through Marriage	Patricia Yeowart	49
Reborn	Nicola Linfield	50
Looking On	Glynis A Foster	50

Water Sports Maestro	Daphne Richards	51
Yacht Race On Boating Lake	Freda Grieve	52
Sporting Chance	Margarette L Damsell	53
Virtually Swimming	Rosa Barbary	53
Water Baby	Angela Tomlinson	54
The Wave	Chris Leesmith	54
Why Do They Do It?	Beryl Jones	55
The Big Splash	Isobel Clanfield	56
Slip Up In Scuba School	Louise Needham	57
Making A Splash	Caroline Brankin	57
The Edge	Kath Pigdon	58
The Day I Belly-Flopped	Christopher A J Evans	59
Swimming Memories	Antoinette Spooner	59
Another Swim Disappointment?	C M Vickers	60
	Wendi Hudson	61
Slalom At Appletreewick	Ken Langford	62
Born To Dream	Kay Spurr	63
Open Boating ABC	Liz Beard	64
From Creeks To Crests	Peter R Lander	65
Ode To The Junior Squad	Chris Muir	66
Swimming	Paul Corrigan	66
A Reluctant Water Baby	Karen E Poad	67
The Fool In The Pool	Brita Bevis	68
A Fishy Army	Muriel R Wrigley	69
The Water Baby	Yan Parlan	69
The End	David Daymond	70
First Day Swimmer	Pamela Gibson	71
The Lesson	Patricia J Castle	72
Don't Forget Your Arm Bands!	Tim Gough	72
J B Vessel	James Stewart	73
The Ex Descent	Julie Playfoot	74
Taking The Plunge	Merril Morgan	75
Gems To Seek	Margaret Jackson	76
Swimming Lesson	Evelyn M Harding	76
Wind Surfing	Linda Casey	77

The Channel Swimmer	Peter Haines	78
Canoeing Is Life	Chris Paton	79
Have No Fear	Cheryl McGowan	79
Hippopoto-Me	Rhoda Glanville	79
Ski Ride	Barbara Fosh	80
First Swim	Dawn Lesley Owen	81
Adrenaline Rider	Arfur Mo	81
The Swimmer	Geoff Jeffries	82
Splash	Hannah Wharton	83
Learning To Swim	Sheena Probert	84
Another Shore	Alan Noble	84
Chris's Dilemma	Bob Durnan	85
Liquid Games	Howard Riley	86
In My Boat, I Long	Mark Davidson	86
Canoeing At Symonds Yat	Rachel Walker	87
Canoeing	P Griffin	87
Sitting On The Bank	John Milliner	88
The Rapid	Ron Brown	89
My Brother's Diving Adventure Off The South Coast	Julia Wallis-Bradford	90
In At The Deep End	John W Skepper	91
A Day At The Seaside	Barbara Eyre	92
The Surfer	James Jarvis	92
Collecting The Sunday Paper In Cowal	Mhairi Dwight	93
Friday Street Kitchen	Trish Birtill	94
A Non-Swimmer With Friends	Rowena Shepherd	94
The Swimming Lesson	V C Ball	95
Floating	Suzy Messenger	96
Lovely Day For A Swim	Prudence Bates	96
Thinking Over Mary's Invitation	Eileen Holt	97
PBK 20	Idris Owen	97
In At The Deep End	Mary Johnson	98
Learning With Play	Monica Rehill	99

The Dive	Josie Minton	100
Lullaby	Angela Matheson	100
Ocean Adventure	Marlene Peckham	101
Laying-Up	Peter Fenwick	102
Ode To A Windsurfer	Jemima Norman	103
Sychronised Swimming	Esther Rehill	104
The Diver	Elizabeth Camp	104
In The Pool	Geoff Skellon	105
Surfing	Caroline Robinson	105
Crystal Waters	Carolyn Finch	106
Oh To Be In The Water	Melanie Burgess	106
A Quick Fall In The Swimming Pool	Gemma Daniel	107
Cowes Week	Trevor Read	108
Young At Heart	Ethel Hatfield	108
Water Phobia	Barbara Harrison	109
Winter Swimming	William M Jones	110
Sun, Sea And Sewage	Affrug	111
Watersport	Iris Selly	112
The First Swimming Lesson	Paul Perry	112
Fighting The Flab	Shabnam Walji	113
Chaqu'un	Sue Holtom	114
Splashing Around I Nearly Drowned	Russell Pengelly	115
Wave Machine	Victoria Clark	115
Landlubber Booby	Marjorie Spark	116
The Swimmer	Kenny McPhee	117
Come On Grandad	Mary Williams	118
Sporting Challenge	Patricia Belfield	118
Wave Power	Moira Brabender	119
Escape	Marie Hodgman	120
Messing About	Margaret Carter	120
School Diving Competition	Sean Flanagan	121
Age Is No Barrier	Tony Hughes-Southwart	122
Watersports	Janette Campbell	123
I Have A Dog	Peter Hassall	123

Title	Author	Page
Ode To A Banana Boat	Tracey Thomson	124
Not Swimming - Drowning	Thomas A Rattray	124
Ode To Diana	Katherine A Ford	125
Boating	Eileen Handley	126
Freestyle	Matt Pearson	127
Sea-Borne	William Edward Lewis (Jr)	127
Swimming Lesson	Sonia Griffiths	128
An Awful Man	Debbie McQuiston	129
Treasure Seekers	S V Smy	130
Swimming	Marie-Therese H Russell	131
High On A Wave	Michael John Swain	132
Fish Eye View	David McRonald	132
In The Swim	A Bytheway	133
Frogman	A Mac Gábann	134
Swimming Lessons	Alison Jacobs	134
Ocean Meditation	Daniel Jones	135
Surfing City	Gena K Crawford	136
Mum's A Real Beach Bum	Kim Bettley	137
A Gentle Form Of Sport	P A Beard	138
Water Baby I'm Not!	Elaine Lochè	139
Summer Days By The River	Claire Young	139
High Dive	Katie Hart	140
Calling All Water Babies - Sporty Thoughts!	Traceyanne Chafer	140
Aqua Summer	Lynda Devereux	141
Big Toe Day	Peggy Ruth Banks	142
Bikini Bimbo	Sherrlee Blythin	143
Just Ain't For Me	Clive Cornwall	143
The Windsurfer	L B Yates	144
The Dive	Mark Tettenborn	144
Beauty Beneath The Sea	Sheila MacDonald	145
Under The Waves	Melanie Unsworth	145
Water Wonderful World	K A Travis	146
Beach Blues	James E B Smith	147

Why Can't I Swim	Jeanette Gaffney	148
Swimming	Margery Richards	148
Messing About On The River	B Gates	149
The King Pool Of The River Of Milk	Kathleen Schmidt	150
Be Safe	Philip E Cox	150
Water	'Bunny' Newman	151
The Sea The Sea	Hal Cheetham	152
Come To The Pool	Catherine Long	153
Below The Surface	Ruth L Ironside	154
Surf Versus Me	Jil Bramhall	155
The Fanatic	Robert Lumsden	156
Surfing	Sybil Sibthorpe	157
Bobbing About In The River!	Angela Rogerson	158
Try A Snorkel Or Two!	Elizabeth M Sudder	159
Watersprite	Dorothy Neil	160
Maybe	L R Frost	160
Pride Comes Before A Plunge	Dorothy White	161
Going Down	Jayne Hilary Lowry	162
Geared Up	L Medcalf	163
Daddy's Gone Out Diving	Michelle Devine	164
Orca-Envy	Marne Eric Watts	165
Embarrassing Moment	Dawn Stangi	165
The Galleon	Wayne Ford	166
Never Too Late To Learn	J Walters	167
Farne Island Dive	C Smith	168
Untitled	Pat Cunliffe	169
The Beauty Of The Sea	Kirsty MacDougall	170
Early Morning Dive	Valerie Sheldon	171
The Reef	Deborah Edge	172
The Waters Of Avalon	Richard J Heads	173
Don't Stop Breathing	Kerry Lee	174
Sunken Dreams	Mick Devine	175
In Too Deep	Suzy Walsh	176
Dive	Keith Pritchett	177

Diving Free	Ann Guilder	178
Notice Of A New Navigational Hazard In Channel	The Stowting Bard	179
Dive Fever	Ian Geraint Jones	180
Deep Sea Diver	W V Ponting	181
First Nerves	C Meredith	182

WATER, SUN, BOAT AND SKIS

To do this sport, I need all of these,
First I try on the boom,
It gets me skiing very soon,
Then I try on the long line,
But I do not get up every time,
I keep on trying, I won't give in,
I will eventually stop falling in,
Now I'm up on skis at last,
Soon I'll be going very fast,
Several times around the lake,
At last I'm learning to cross the wake,
What's the next thing I can do,
Ski on one, not on two,
On the boom again I go,
It's hard to balance on one you know,
Wobbly and unsteady to start,
With a few tries I've mastered the art,
It's now time to try dropping one ski,
I've done it at last, but it wasn't easy,
Now I can mono on one ski,
The next thing is the deep water start for me,
It took me several times to do,
But now I enjoy it better than two,
I think I'll give the slalom course a miss,
I'll try the tricks instead of this,
It's such a funny thing to do,
Slipping and sliding, but great fun too,
The jump is the last thing on my list,
But afraid I'm just not brave enough for this.

S A Hills

THE WAVE

Sitting here, transfixed by your beauty, in awe of your power,
                              as the sun sets you beckon me,
I can feel your warm breath, as you open your mouth wide, you roar
    like a lion, the foam dripping from your lips glistens in the sunlight.
The spray twinkles like a million stars, you are the king of all,
                                        untameable, unstoppable.
Again you roar louder, excitement builds within me, adrenaline rushes
                          through my veins,
And the sweet salty smell of your breath fills the air, and makes me heady.
Anticipation grips me, a distant fear twists the inside of my stomach,
            as the whole sweet experience I cannot deny myself.
I'm drawn, like a magnet of thrills, to your den, and your territory.
I choose my moment, you are asleep for a short time, or so I thought,
                          then you awaken with great ferocity,
I feel so small and humble, like a rag doll in a rinse cycle; trapped in
                                      your boiling cauldron.
I fight to gain control, and momentarily I win, I vow to myself that I
      will be the victor in our never ending battles and skirmishes,
This time I am ready, in a brief moment of euphoria I escape your clutches,
Carefully I perform some clown like tricks in your path, as if teasing
                and daring you into some higher form of retribution.
Swiftly I dance around your gaping mouth, the moisture forming droplets
          like teeth, being careful not to get snapped at or sucked in.
Again I turn to face you like a matador, but even though its bitingly cold,
                              and the air holds sombre chill,
Sweat forms on my brow, part fear and exertion, but mostly in
                    anticipation of the next round still to come.
Although I try to hurt you, with turns even sharper, like the twist of an
    assassin's knife, your scars miraculously disappear, in the fading twilight.
Like a chameleon you change your moods and colours, sometimes calm
                                          and blue,
And others like today you are white green and ferocious, devouring all that
                                      stands in your way.
Momentarily I'm lost daydreaming, engulfed in your power,
You seize your opportunity and send me hurtling with effortless ease,
                through the air with a thoughtless sweep,

Your cold wet presence everywhere, in my ears in my eyes, you swipe
                                                                and maul,
And try to tear the clothes from my tired battered body, as I try to escape.
As I clamber up the stony open expanse, that I call a beach, I look
                        back on the carnage, I once proudly called my kit.
But although you've won this battle, its not the end of the war, but one
               thing that I know deep down, I'll be back next week for more.

Mark A Hagerty

WHY DO WE DO IT?

The bloody jetty's bloody cold,
This bloody suit is bloody old,
It's full of holes and bloody thin,
The bloody water pours right in.
The bloody queue is five miles long,
The bloody slalom course is wrong,
Half the bloody buoys have sunk,
The guy in charge is bloody drunk.
The rubber binding's bloody tight,
And I don't feel too bloody bright,
The bloody judge is half awake,
I know I cleared that bloody wake.
The bloody jump is out of line,
The bloody sun won't bloody shine.
All year long I've tried and tried,
I've swallowed all my bloody pride,
What kind of sport do you call this?
A bloody metamorphosis!
But when all's said and bloody done.
This bloody sport is still such fun
To be asked if I'll give up next year
Is *sacrilege!*. . . No bloody fear!

Judy Crane

WATER-SKI BUDDIES

It started in the changing rooms.
My first challenge get the wetsuit on!
Wiggle, wiggle, pull and push, twenty minutes
Later there I've won.

Stepping in your breath has gone,
The waters cold but not for long.
Both hands tightly on the handle, skis
Seem right now don't go wrong.

Look down fall down that's what they tell.
The boats all ready the rope is tight,
My buddies are waiting - 'Hit it' I yell!

My arms are coming out of their sockets
My legs are parting in different directions
Like Rockets!
The water is up my nose and in my eyes, oops in the
Water - What a surprise !

Where am I ? Where's everyone gone ?
'Well done you nearly did it', 'Do you want to do it again '?
'Keep your legs together, head up, arms straight,
You'll be up this time and around the lake'.

Look down fall down that's what they tell.
The boats all ready the rope is tight,
My buddies are waiting - 'Hit it' ; I yell!

Something's different, I can tell
I'm standing up - 'Come on' they yell
That's it I've done it, I'm on two skis
Proud as punch and thanks to these; - Marc, Pete and Kate

Wendi Turner

SKI FEVER

I must go down to ski again, under the smoke-filled sky;
And all I ask is a strong boat and a rope to pull me by;
And the ski's kick and the fowl's pong, and the white caps breaking;
And a green stench on the lake's face, and the swan's neck shaking.

I must go down to ski again, for the call of the slalom course
Is a clear call, and a strong call, when you're pulling like a horse;
And all I ask is a windless day, with the sunshine exquisite;
And an open loo for the one and two, on the *weekday* visit.

I must go down to ski again, when life's long tale is told,
And the Commodore says ' Come in my friend, out of the festering cold'
And all I ask if they've skis up there, (it gives me cause to wonder)
I'll drag my butt through that slalom course in the wide blue yonder!

O R Ballard

IN AT THE DEEP END

I remember when Bob took us swimming,
We'd go down to Barrow Baths,
I didn't really enjoy it,
But Bob and our Steve had some laughs,
They used to think it was funny,
Just because I couldn't swim,
They'd treat me really rotten,
One day, they just threw me in,
Somehow I managed to struggle,
To get myself backed to the side,
I was so upset and frightened,
They both really hurt my pride,
After that things did get better,
They just left me well alone,
Then one day I amazed them,
I learnt to swim all on my own.

Kazzie Ingram

H2 O MY GOD!

Firstly slip into your neoprene skin
And prepare to produce some adrenaline
180's, 360's, flips and side slides
Are displayed on two bubbling boat wake tides
Big fun and impressive's the event of tricking
The others as well are really butt kicking!

Barefooting's a sport for the seriously insane
Could you stand on the roof of a speeding train?
That's the feeling you get, it's completely spine chilling
Don't think of a fall, or your guts will be spilling.

If that's not enough, then zig zag the course
Technique is quite simple, use pure brute force!
Then you can try something really heart pumping
You can fly through the air whilst water-ski jumping
Attack that ramp with guts and aggression
If you land in one piece, you've achieved your mission.

Waterskiing's no craze, it's an addictive passion
With you for life, it's no phase and no fashion.

Joyce Barclay

WATERWAYS

Miles and miles of waterways,
A legacy of yesterdays,
Harder slower pace of life,
When a bargee, and his wife,
Worked side by side with family to,
Carrying cargo for folk like you.

Now we use them just for pleasure,
A wonderful way to spend our leisure.
What better way is there to unwind,
From the dreary daily grind,
Then slowly cruising on our way,
Or sitting fishing for a day?

G W Bailey

WINDSURFING

The song of the sea
is to be free
to skip over the waves
at an angle,
sometimes our feet dangle
between the mist and the spray
in the cool azure sea.
To master the art
reject from the start
this being is me
but some other knight
as jousting is free
with the sea.
Sudden stones and shells,
the mighty swells
as the wind propels
our dizzying feet
until suddenly spent
the tremors cease
we are at our ease
gently cushioned by the breeze.

Joan Hands

COME FOLLOW

Come follow me down into the sea
And you will see wondrous things
Beneath the waves we'll find the caves
Where many fish do go
And the silence shouts about us
Each one puts on its show
Colours mingle in to coloured rainbows
for our eyes alone.
Flitting and darting like jewels
Up to the cove dome.
Giving us things to talk and think about
All the way home.
For I am old and I've seen it all before.
You are so young
For you I've opened up a new door
So after today it can now never be
When you look out with different eyes
Will you - just see the sea.

Winifred Wardle

DEEP IN A WORLD OF WONDER

Under the water I'd be,
Diving to and fro just like the
fish in the sea.
Dolphins jump high,
I dive low to see all the
beauty down below.
Old myths of the sea,
The treasures I see.
Lost below I am not afraid
feeling of loneliness
Has gone away.

Sarah Tahir

SWIMMING WITH STYLE

Every time I suggest going swimming,
My wife starts on about slimming,
'If I was slim,' she would say,
'This swimsuit would fit me the right way,
Instead of hugging all my trimmings'

When we eventually make it to the pool,
She'll just lay by the side looking cool,
Wearing her dark shades,
She'll lay and she'll gaze,
If you ask me she looks like a fool.

Now, the other day I got her in the water,
She couldn't swim that well so I taught her,
She screamed for a while,
But soon showed some style,
And was swimming just as she oughta.

She was swimming with plenty of grace,
And her legs were going at some pace,
She didn't see me go under,
All I heard was a thunder,
And her legs ended up smack in my face.

She quoted, 'This isn't as bad as I thought,
I haven't yet once got distraught,
This really suits me,
We should come regularly,
It's a wonderful water sport.'

Richard Bright

SHARK!

At our school swimming lesson
It's all such a lark !
When someone's on the diving - board
And someone else yells: *'Shark!'*
The person standing up there
Nervously looking down
Doesn't really believe it
But nonetheless give a frown.
There's that extra little shake of the knees,
As they grimly step up to the edge.
They can't help thinking that one
Snap of Shark's jaws and they're dead!
They know that there's no way
That a shark could be in the pool.
But they start to imagine the beady black eyes
And try not to lose their cool.
They lean and dive in bravely,
Thinking they've beaten the trap.
But to everyone's amazement,
The great beast's jaws go ... *snap!*
A great white in the water ? !
It really was most unexpected.
It somehow got through the filter
And slipped in undetected!

Lynda Blagg

WATER DANGERS

Watersport is the name
Getting wet is the game.

Swimming, diving, surfing too,
Is a must for you.

It's the in thing, so learn to swim.
Don't just go and dive straight in.

Don't be daft, do not dither,
Stay away from the river.

Don't be a fool, in the pool
That's the important golden rule.

Tony Williams

SWIMMING LESSONS

They taught us to swim at Dunn Street school
The lessons were fun, in that big, heated pool
We fooled and joked about, not caring
While Meadows, the teacher, took to despairing

One lesson, we were learning to dive
And being clever, my mate Clive
Dived from the board at the upper-most height
While everyone else looked on in fright

The dive was not bad, the landing, rotten
And Clive took his time coming up from the bottom
After a minute, Meadows was there
As he made for the lad, all we did was stare

He pulled our Clive out onto the side
Everyone thought that our mate had died!
But Meadows had the inspiration
To give him artificial resuscitation

Our Clive, he coughed, and then he spluttered
And with a gasping breath he uttered
'Marks out of ten - what have I got?'
'For daftness', said Meadows, 'I'd give you a lot!'

At the next swimming lesson, we paid attention
As Meadows felt the need to mention
How fooling about in the water, he said
Was stupid, 'cause someone might end up dead!

Margaret Sanderson

WELL DID YOU EVER

Did you ever
See the forecast
For your local beach
Force 5 westerly
Its going to be a peach

Did you ever
Load your gear
Onto the roof rack of your car
To drive the 50 miles or so
It never seems that far

Did you ever
Get that feeling
The adrenaline rush
The sea spread out before you
White horses and such mush

Did you ever
Rig up faster
Than a cat climbs up a tree
Get into your wet suit
And forget to have a pee

Did you ever
Go out sailing
When the wind was just too light
And struggle back to safety
Not giving up the fight

Did you ever
Meet that flash git
With the very silly grin
'You should have been here yesterday'
Says he 'That's when you should have been!'

Ben Dearnley

PARLAIZ ANGLAIS

Me and Jean were going to be famous, we decided to swim the Channel!
On our old globe of the world it was only half an inch wide?
If we went into training for a month we could do it if we tried.
We'd seen on 'Pathe' news of this swimmer covered in fat, we took some lard
out of mum's pantry, we'd have to make do with that!
We ate porridge every morning, drank cocoa every night, did the breast
Stroke laid in bed, did press ups holding the cat!
We'd reached up to twenty lengths in the deep end of the local baths,
Under water, on top of it, beware anyone crossing our paths!
Now we had to learn French! My dad was there in the war, we asked 'Will
you teach us to talk French? 'He looked at mum and blushed, 'Whatever for?'
Mum gave us one of her 'funny' looks, 'We don't discuss that trip to France,
No good you hidin' behind that paper, you'd be off like a shot, given a chance!'
We asked our teacher to teach us a few words, to parlaiz vous Francais,
She said she was delighted, 'It will come in useful one day'.
Jean's dad was going to Filey, perfect! We'd start our channel swim from there?
Waved goodbye, ran to the sea, got lard all stuck in my hair!
The water was cold, the sun didn't shine, Jean began to turn blue.
'I think we'll do it another day, I'm freezin', how about you?'
We spent all our savings on real fish and chips, hot tea, waited for her
dad to drive us in his car,
Mum asked us ' How was Filey love, was the sea cold? Did you swim very far?'
To this day we never told her of our quest to be in the hall of fame,
Even though we both speak French it will never be the same? Us arriving
Cold and covered in lard upon that alien shore to shouts and cheers of
'Hooray!'
And us, the intrepid Channel swimmers asking, 'Do you Parlaiz Anglais?'!

Joyce M Hefti-Whitney

MY FIRST SKI

A Sunday evening in July
as once again we're driving by.
I've seen them every time we pass,
but never had the chance.

But now at last my day has come;
we stop; go in; await the fun.
'The open day of '95';
they say we'll all succeed.

The wet suit damp, I stretch and pull
'Til half way on, it looks quite full.
With every part of me clamped tight
I'm feeling rather numb.

Outside I step, if step describes
the way I move, this suit inside.
I waddle to the water's edge
to sit and watch and wait.

Out on the water boats speed by
and skiers jump to ski the sky.
Some cross the wave they call 'the wake';
I think it might be mine.

My turn is close. The coach calls out
and through my mind flows every doubt.
The skis go on and ski vest too.
It's now or never time.

The water's warm; what a relief!
I'm floating there in disbelief.
The rope goes tight. I tuck up small
and then I feel the pull.

The water past me starts to rush,
then more and more the waters gush,
my arms pulled hard, my knees bent tight,
then joy of joy, I'm up!

Well, not quite up but half way there,
I crouch while water sprays the air.
Then as my legs begin to stand
I hit the water. 'Splash.'

Andrew Whale

SEAWARD BOUND

We left Dartmouth
and punched out,
an hour before
the top of the tide.

Past the castle
and
the fairway buoys,
on to the Mewstones.

Still no wind
we leave the engine on:
'Rumpty Thump'
'Thumpty Rump'.

We looked at the chart,
plotted our course
and
set 'Ernie' up.

With a 'Whirr'!
And a 'Grr',
he pointed our nose
into

the quiet,
welcoming,
husky,
dusk.

Richard Saunders

SEA SONG

And slowly I sink beneath the waves
As darkness comes obscuring now,
Sea wrack and bladder pass me by
as I my descending course pursue.
I sink intent upon the deep
that dim engulfing realm of time.
Too long I struggled for the light
Striven too hard to hear the strain
of that lost music; lost again
in the distemper of the night.
Too long have I tried to catch the sun
to hold the orb within my heart,
the bitter winter's rain
has torn all that apart.
As slowly I sink beneath the waves
the silence
                      overwhelming now,
Direction lost, beyond control,
I pass beyond the world of sight
and slide into perpetual night.

Peter Francis

DIVERS' PARADISE

Far-off lands and coral seas
Silver sands and tropic breeze.

Beneath the waves a myriad hue
Jewelled fish and aqua blue.

Corals paint the back-drop scene
With domes and pinnacles between.

Sea fans flex as waters swirl
Feather stars their arms unfurl.

Dark caves give refuge from daylight
'Til twilight ushers in the night.

All this and more delights our eyes
As vivid colours hypnotise.

The wonders of the deep entice -
This is a divers' paradise.

Vicki Billings

SUNRISE SAILING

The sound, the smell, the taste, the atmosphere
Sun raising and fresh, on a beach I hold so dear
Light breeze and sail flap, sheets pulled in taught,
Foresail bellows, then as she fills, mast and rigging retort.

So slowly at first, with great sense of expectancy,
Then, the first ripple as bow breaks thu' and sets you free.
Pull in the slack, adjust and settle down,
Throwing down the surplus sheet,
as you bring her steady round.

Then catch a glimpse as the shore slips slowly by,
now gathering momentum, you heave a subconscious sigh.
Releasing all the tension, mind now on other things,
cutting through the water, Oh! how my soul it sings.

Then that special moment, as running with the wind,
standing out on the gunwale, spray in face and find
that along with the shore now, all stress is left behind,
lungs so full of freshness, the air as sweet as wine.

Out into the sunrise, to see what we shall find
invigorating as the physical overpowers the mind,
eventually to return but, not quite as before,
tired, but body, mind and soul demanding more and more.

P A Robbins

PURE EXTREME

Sun rise high,
Sea breeze await.
White horses dance, in far distant waves.
Boards await on beaches around.
In search for wind and wave to jump
In the pure extreme.
The beach start's ago.
The wind in my hair, sea spray in my face,
Warm water's a blue, and crystal clear.
Swift moves with the board, that slices the wave,
That sends about, like butterfly's on wing.
A tack, a gybe, and even a chop, as wave's too
Small for the pure extreme.
As I gybe my last time, and the sun sets behind,
And the red sky above, it's time to head back, as
Sands await.
As I unrig and look beyond, may be tomorrow,
I will return, for that pure extreme.

Craig Alan Hornby

THE SEA SURVIVES

Descending down a lonely line
      to find a place
         untouched by time
Leaving more than footprints in the sand
A world not ours shaped by our hand.

An old ships bones become a reef
      Life comes from death
         and confirms our belief.
We enter the sea a world different from ours
To cherish its beauty
and are held by its powers.

Sewage, oil and rubbish there by the ton.
      Till the waters turn black
      and are covered by scum
We look on ourselves as guardians of the sea
Without man, the sea thrives.
But with out Oceans
Can we?

David Ball

BEGINNER

Standing in the changing room,
Trying to put on my kit,
Are you sure this wetsuit is my size ?,
I can't get my fat to fit.

Finally it's on and done up,
I think my heads going to burst,
I'm having trouble walking,
I feel I need to ski first.

Wooden planks are stuck on my feet,
Life jacket strapped to my chest,
An ungainly entry to the water,
I'm told to just do my best.

I'm knackered from all this exertion,
Then suddenly I'm up on my skis,
Oh brother, oh boy what a feeling,
Can I do it again tomorrow please.

Who cares if my wetsuit's glued on,
Who cares if my feet feel like ice,
I've skied for the first time ever,
I didn't know anything could be so nice.

Helen Mallourides

THE DIVE

Deep down in the ocean where it's dark
Live manta rays and many breeds of shark
Black tip, white tip, some without a mark
Each whose bite is worse than his bark.

Down the reef wall from the surface blue
Corals every conceivable hue
Thronged with reef fish come into our view
Fish for cleaner wrasse form a queue.

Weird fishes are seen as we drift down
Corals attacked by the thorned crown
Devoured by starfish which makes us frown
Anemones guarded by clown.

At thirty metres no plants are seen
The animal world down here reigns supreme
Lost are the colours red, pink and green
Everything blue as in a dream.

Right down to the bottom for a sight
A large grey shape causes us quite a fright
A symbol of vast power and might
Those large white teeth seeking a bite.

Close to the reef wall we stop and stare
No violent movements, we must take care
Of narcosis we must be aware
A thrilling time for those who dare.

Such a dive nothing else can transcend
But all too soon it must come to an end
Up the reef wall we now must ascend
Not too fast, must not get a bend.

Breaking the surface, we meet the sun
And the glorious dive is nearly done
The boat comes towards us at a run
But what a dive and oh what fun!

Roy Prentice

I CAN SWIM

When I retired from teaching I could swim.
Well, not the kind of swimming where you skim
Across the water, head down, flashing arms around,
But the swimming where one's head's very firmly found
Well above the water, with the face and eyes quite clear,
With white stretch cap upon the hair in case a splash comes near!
So my breast stroke was a model of propriety, quite prim,
And never in a month of Sundays did I think of jumping in!

Then I retired and went to lessons in my local swimming pool.
I did whatever I was asked of, as the teacher made the rules!
I learnt to swim beneath the water, through a hoop and pick up bricks,
I even did a sort of crawl with very vigorous leg kicks!
So I learnt diving and 'survival' and to jump I'd even try!
Though it was just as well they'd swimming wear if they were passing by!

I now have over twenty badges proudly on the kitchen wall.
Who cares if they say 'adult swim', for it's the metres they recall!
I've got a 'challenge' and 'endeavour' and I even swam a mile!
Now I work for 'swim fit' badges too and I do it in great style!

How I love my swimming lessons, they're a highlight of my week!
It's not swimming fame and fortune that in old age I will seek,
It's the joy I have from swimming now retirement time is here
And I swim with my grandchildren, never showing any fear -

'Cause I *can swim!*

Sheila E Harvey

UNDERWATER

There is a place, beyond the shingle strand,
Where, deep in the cool green fastness of the sea,
The flashing forms of fishes weave above the silver sand.
Behind the headland, in the lee,
Caressed by currents, weed fronds wave and twirl,
Flower - like, the sea anemones spread and furl.
Farther from the rocky Cornish shore
Thirteen fathoms below boundary of sea and sky
Indigo are the depths, seldom seen by man before.
By virtue of water - glider, the esoteric joy to fly
Is known to us, swishing through the pellucid streams
Motion is smooth, breathing tubes flutter, the scene unfolds.
Above, midst a multitude of sounds a seabird screams.
Mute now, torn and broken with shattered holds
A ship has lain since the night of bravery years ago
Quiet, except for the gentle tinkle of bubbles.
Pale violet, green and rose, sea - urchins are all aglow
Forward and back, orange and blue, a cuckoo wrasse doubles.

K G Brough

HESITANT

I stand there rather hesitant
It looks so very deep
Is anybody watching me
I turn and have a peep

My knees are knocking frantically
I don't know if I should
Perhaps with a life jacket
Maybe then I could

I will be brave I'll do it
My feet go in right now
I am in up to my kneecaps
I am such a brave brave gal!

The water comes up higher
Promise not to laugh
I've got this fear of drowning
But I am only in the bath.

Angela Pearson

NO PAIN!

I remembered that as a child I loved to swim,
So I took it up again to keep myself trim,
I bought a new costume at a bargain price,
But I had to take it back not once but twice,
Two sizes later and I found one that fit,
Although it took me ten minutes to squeeze into it,
The water gave me goose bumps when I jumped in,
So to warm myself up I started to swim,
I sank and swallowed a gallon of water or more,
When I came up my eyes were bloodshot and sore,
I tried again and this time I was doing OK,
When a man swimming by got in my way,
The next thing I knew I was gazing at arms and legs,
Distorted faces wearing goggles and nose pegs,
I rested to think but I did not have long,
Because I had to find out what I was doing wrong,
With breathless determination I would not be satisfied,
Until I could swim smoothly from side to side,
After several more attempts I could do it at last,
I glided through the water and I was fast,
But in the changing room I noticed my aching limbs,
I was exhausted but I had enjoyed my swim,
That was last year and I have been every week since,
But the thought of that day still makes me wince.

Kathleen Speed

I PREFER PUDDLES

I don't like watersports
of any sorts,
just simply because I cannot swim,
and I don't like getting wet.
The funny part about it all
is, I love to splash about in the rain
with my brolly and wellies.
I am not a water baby
and regret never learning to swim,
but I love the puddles
and wish I could jump in.
I love the patterns in the pavements
after the rain has been
but most of all I love
what God made above
His lovely rainbow.

R Medland

DREAMS

If only you could dream as I have dreamt,
Of the endless oceans,
Of the endless depths,
Of the endless love of the dolphins,
Of the endless embrace of the whales,
And of my own endless peace,
I have dreamt these endless dreams,
And I hope never to awake from them,
For they keep me alive,
They are like air in the lungs,
And water in the gills,
Like feathers in the sky,
And like the voice from an animal's cry.

Selina Patel

SIMON AT SIX

Simon was gentle and loving
And God gave him such a nice smile.
His brother named Tim was eleven.
Quite clever and did things in style.

He sang in the choir each Sunday
And sometimes he acted in shows.
He didn't have nerves too often
And was good at most things he chose.

None of this bothered young Simon.
At six he had time on his side.
Mummy was there to encourage
And in his achievements take pride.

Saturdays he went to swimming
With mummy and Bert his dear friend.
Still he was just a bit cautious
And never went near the deep end.

First he had fun simply splashing
Though he tried very hard to swim.
One day with Timothy missing
Came a chance that seemed made for him.

He climbed an inflatable island
And cheerfully smiled when he fell.
Then back to the start he clambered
Till proudly a moment to tell.

For he reached the end so happy
Then jumped off just where it was deep.
So Simon found himself swimming
And that night contented would sleep.

John Christopher Cole

MEMORIES OF THE SCHOOL GALA

All were there, mam, Aunty Peggy, and big sister
Clare,
There's smug smiling Sue, swims like a fish
And knows it too.
I cannot come last, I mustn't dare, they'd
Be so disappointed, it just wouldn't be fair
Mam said though, it's not the winning, it's
The taking part.
All must be sporting, and accept the results
With good spirit and heart.
Second or third, I wouldn't mind, as long as
I am not lagging behind.
There's Mrs Dawson, with the whistle, and
We're all on our marks.
Fourth's not so bad, anyhow I did beat
Mary Sparks.
Now it's off home for me, and mam's even
Promised some tasty treat.
Jam tarts with our 4 o'clock afternoon
Tea.

Christine Corbett

WATER WORSHIP

Water, water everywhere
But not a drop to swim in
Canoeists, surfers, motorboats
And semi-naked women
To find a spot where they are not
Gets harder every year
So I'll join them now and show them how
To be a granddad water skier

Pete Harrison

THE SEA URCHINS

We call our son and his pals the sea urchins,
For the best waves they never stop their searchings,
When the weather is bad and the sea is rough,
Our sea urchin and his siblings just can't get enough,
We wouldn't venture in or even dip a toe,
Temperature is off the gauge at least five below,
Our worries over tides currents and pollution levels,
Doesn't appear to deter this hardy bunch of sea-devils,
Often we insist that they don't take for granted the sea,
It can quickly turn from friend to foe and become your enemy,
We hear their nonchalant talk it's all so matter of fact,
It's as if with the sea they have this special pact,
Killjoys we are not, neither poets of doom,
But for complacency at sea there is never any room,
To keep things in perspective and on a brighter note,
We often go down to the beach and watch the urchins float,
Recently we trooped off to the distant bay at Kimmeridge,
Rain, wind and angry sea married to temperatures from the fridge,
Remote and bleak are words that spring to mind,
Also desolate and isolated and that is being kind,
On that day the sea contained its secrets and its dignity,
As the boarders nerve and bravado paled to insignificance,
Conquering Kimmeridge was deferred, put on hold,
Another day another time for that story to unfold,
So it's back to Bournemouth their own golden patch,
Paddling out past the pier for the shore-bound waves to catch,
Speeding through the barrel, gracefully they glide,
Hopefully arriving in one piece on the other side,
Servants of the sea, riders of the waves,
Devotees of the surf, these body boarding slaves.

Peter Littlefield

GOD BLESS THE RNLI

They've sailed the coastlines of Britain
since the year eighteen twenty and four.
It is well over one hundred thousand
that have been brought back safely to shore.
Now anyone venturing out on our seas
knows a lifeboat is somewhere nearby:
standing ready and waiting emergency calls
is a crew of the RNLI.

> From all those who sail the oceans
> to land all the much needed food;
> to those who go boating for pleasure,
> but who may leave us thinking them fools;
> to them that despite valiant effort
> don't keep themselves up in the sky;
> they all depend on the brave volunteers
> of the faithful RNLI

Yes they step out upon yonder oceans
whenever they hear distant cries.
And they go to all lengths to save them
and make sure and firm their reply.
Though the waters that wash this small island
have kept the mortality high,
on the seas round our coast in Britain we boast
of the courage of the RNLI.

> So thanks to the ones that go asking
> and thanks to the ones that respond;
> and thanks too to those who go rattling
> the boxes that make up the funds.
> On behalf of the thousands they rescue
> and the many who may still rely
> on the guts and commitment of any
> who serve in the RNLI.

Boris

HYPERACTIVE BATHING

Every night at half past six
He's in the bath it's time for tricks
I think he does it all for kicks
I wish he'd play with building bricks
He ducks his head and holds his breath
Sometimes until he's near his death
He then jumps up and gasps for air
Suds clinging to his bright red hair
Sliding down the slanty end
Whizzing towards the taps
There's ducks and sponges everywhere
The place is full of traps
Out of the bath and into the sink
Whenever he's caught he's getting a drink
It doesn't take him long to think
Of another excuse to tickle you pink
He never knows just what to do
He'll fiddle with the hair shampoo
You shout until your face is blue
But it still ends up going down the loo
Facecloths usually last a day
They all end up being flushed away
Tomorrow is another day
He'll settle down I hope and pray
My nerves are wrecked the wife's are too
But all he does is stare at you
That devilish laugh many hearts has won
He's David McCrudden our youngest son.

David Gibbons

MY FIRST LESSON

It's 3 pm, the swimming lesson must begin.
My heart is thudding, my chest within.
I'm not the bravest in this class of mine,
Please let the fear of water soon decline.

First lesson ever, that was a quick half hour,
Time now to enjoy a nice hot shower.
Breast stroke, back stroke or front crawl,
I'll conquer one if not them all.

Ten weeks on, I can swim quite well,
I am proud my tale to tell.
I may never attain Olympic speed,
More important from my fear I have been freed.

Confidence and pleasure I have gained,
Also a higher fitness level I've attained.
So non swimmers make a move,
Book your lessons see your life improve.

Anne Livingstone

UNTITLED

Pulling myself up
From beneath the surface
I opened my eyes
Ears, nose and throat
Allowing everything I felt
To flood through my body

My blood is pumping
As it never has before
And winter is here
To chase away my fears

I breathe the ice cold air
And hold it in for some
Exhaling slowly

As a last attempt
At sanity
I pull my legs up
To my chin
And find myself
Reborn

P Fisher

HOW MUCH FOR A PAIR OF WATER WINGS?

I'd sit at the side and stare at the pool
Speaking to no one I felt such a fool
Those in the pool were in a league of their own
Why I couldn't get there, the answer unknown

I was eleven years old and couldn't swim
No physical reason, no problem in lung or limb
The truth be known, I was scared out of my mind
The courage to climb in, I just couldn't find

Then my teacher who I hated with passion
Came speeding past like speed was going out of fashion
With a nifty little twist and a kick up the bum
Splishing and splashing into the water I had come

After the panic and screaming was all but done
I stood up in the water and found it quite fun
I hadn't drowned or been eaten alive
From learning to swim I really could thrive

Twenty years on, that teacher I thank
My fear of water is well and truly sank
I swim real good and love splashing in the water
Now I'll take great pleasure in teaching the same to my daughter.

Naomi Cooke

SCUBA TOUR

There lies a world of magic
Beneath the ocean blue.
A world of mystic silence
Colours of rainbow hue.

Some say there are mermaids
Merman too I'd say
Although I haven't seen one
Maybe I will some day.

There are so many gullies
For you to explore.
You could never see it all
From any country's shore.

Let me introduce you
To a set of scuba gear.
I will take you by the hand
There is naught to fear.

Just breathe normally
Relax you will enjoy.
There will be you - me
And a surface marker buoy.

There are assorted fish
Shells and pretty grass
Electric eels - sun stars
Hermit crabs - spider crabs.

Velvet crabs - swimming crabs
They all live in the sea.
So come on in I'll show you
Please - follow - me!

Margareth

RED SEA BLUES

My first experience was early one September,
Inside a tiny, safe Mallorcan bay,
With only neons, porgy fish and squid to remember,
No hint of angel, trigger of manta ray.
In waterworld I was the only human
With bubble halo and a rushing in my ears,
A moving underwater fairy herald,
Sharing a new adventure with my peers.
But then there came a greater reef encounter
And now I queue for flights into Eilat,
I reach a new high waiting at the airport
Accepting all that rubber in my case, at luggage check.

Snorkelling replaces all things in its time
But the North Sea clouds the vision with its foggy brine.

Sadly now, happiness is only fish shape,
I long for that old tee shirt on my back,
A plastic card below me on a tape
String. For long stay in the water, I've the knack.
There's gentle competition finding species;
My life list's a hundred and eighty seven.
I find I can just squeeze a week at Christmas.
If I can get away at Easter then that's heaven.
I thought one day the spell it would be broken
But now I've found a partner you see.
We wear identical wetsuits as a token
And at snorkelling she's just as keen as me.

The noise and clean, clear windows on the underground
Recall the turquoise water of the happy hunting ground.

John Hollyer

A STROKE OF LUCK!

I fancied a swim at the swimming baths one day
It was out of season, so there wasn't much to pay
I packed up my cossie, my towel and stuff
And decided that an hour would be long enough

I paid them my money and collected my disc
Put my stuff in a locker, so it wouldn't be at risk
I waded through the footbath to cleanse both my feet
Then smiled at the lifeguard sat high up in his seat

I stood at the side, shivering and cold
And watched all the swimmers both young and old
I began to wonder why I'd come here on a whim
When I knew darned well I hadn't a clue how to swim!

I gingerly lowered myself into the pool
Then grabbed hold of the side, I felt such a fool
I stood gripped in panic at all the water round me
Then realised with relief, it only reached past my knee!

Shivering and cold I knew what I had to do
Move out of this pool as it was for bairns under two
Into the shallow end I quickly went
As a 16 stone woman dived in with intent!

The parting of the water dragged me under too
As struggling and gasping I didn't know what to do
I splashed and I floundered as I swallowed half the pool
The top half of my cossie doesn't get wet as a rule

I gave one last gurgle and thought my end was in sight
When suddenly I was thrust up through the water with might
The 16 stone woman had swam off nice and neat
And the waves from her water had put me back on my feet

The moral of this story is when I feel like a swim
I dismiss it immediately then go off to the gym!

Sharon Goldsmith

THE WATER BABIES' SWIMMING CLUB

Miriam swam: it gave her such a thrill.
For she was lame, and had been very ill;
And that's an extra to arthritic legs
That when she made to move were stiffened pegs
That sharply hurt when ere she tried to walk.
Of that small matter she would never talk.
But it is great to learn to swim and dive
When you have seen the last of seventy-five.

Six-year old Anna could not walk at all,
Or play with other girls, or bounce a ball.
For birth had played her fiendish tricks; and so
Her twisted body simply could not go.
Cumbersome callipers encased her hips,
School was restricted by hospital trips.
She learnt to swim, grew strong, won national cups
Now, on her way to school, where once she slipped
And limped and tripped, with childish joy she *skipped*.

Geoffrey and Jane were born to wheelchair life;
Barbara's spine was like a sharpened knife;
Tom had Down's syndrome; Toby had no arms;
But just protruding fingers 'gainst life's harms.
Philip lacked legs as well, and yet he swam!
One was so young mum brought her in a pram.
One, who lived for this night, was eighty-five.
And swimming made worthwhile the fight to live.

And these and many others were my pride;
We formed a club - *they* took it in their stride,
I, humbly grateful they accepted me,
Did all my puny best to set them free
Of nature's fiendish iniquity.
For forty years it certainly helped *me*.

Ted Cowen

BEAUTIFUL SWIMMER

An old flame, lovely and active
Inside her yellow swimsuit
She's always been attractive
Her smile is still so cute.

And I see that beauty go
To all the same places
And as I watch, I know
She's still winning races.

Her training is superb
My love must slowly simmer
For I must not disturb
The beautiful swimmer.

So powerful, but yet so slim
Such beauty is so rare
And when she comes to swim
I cannot help but stare.

A day spent by the pool
She was good to know
I must have been a fool
To ever let her go.

Andrew Hearn

WETBOB

After work, could one conceive
Upon a balmy summer's eve

A better ending to the day
Than ply the 'wet Bob's' easy way?

In the boat up there a'lying
In the bow with gulls a'crying

Merry wavelets here a'slapping;
Jolly flotsam now a'tapping;

Feel the wash from passing boats
That conjures magic . . being afloat.

The charm of lively water lapping
Near a head almost a'napping

But the thickness of a plank away
To soothe away a weary day.

Ted Herbert

SINK OR SWIM

Splish splash this ain't the bath, quickly someone build me
a raft
There's nothing to it, it's not a craft, get me on dry land up
near the path
My teeth are chattering, there's more than a draught, this pool
looks big and deep, if I get to the middle who knows what I'll meet
I watched Jaws one and two as well, rescue me someone I won't tell
Come on kick your legs you're doing well, easy for you mate, but
for me it's sheer hell, I didn't ask to be part fish, we're only
here at your insist.
Just one more mouthful of this chlorine drink, and I'll do much more
than sink
What's happening now? I'm beginning to shrink, my hands have gone
all crinkly and pink
Oh let me out, this is not for me, find another victim and let
me be
If God had meant me to swim I'm sure he would have supplied me with fins.

Carol Irving

A NEW COSTUME

I guess this is the same old story
We were poor, after the war no glory
But one thing I loved as I grew up
Was swimming, and after Oxo in a cup

My longing was to have a nice bathing costume
And not feel left out in the changing room
But this was not to be at this particular time
I had to make do, at least it was mine.

But I could not rest and leave it there
The older I got, the more into despair,
My mother at the time, did lovely crocheting
Quite pretty it was, she made me a vest in string.

Now one day as fed up as I had been
I showed my temper and made a scene
I want a new costume, to my mother I said
Well what she did next, my face went quite red.

She sewed this crocheted string vest underneath
'There' she said, 'that looks quite chic'.
Into the water I plunged quite deep
Proud of my costume, until out of the water I creep.

It stretched so long and dreadfully baggy
I felt like a sack of potatoes all lumpy and baggy
I crawled to my locker in great disgust
Never again, a new costume is a must.

Pip

WOMAN IN A DINGHY

Young woman in her boat
sitting stock still, as though
she never meant to come on land again.
The sailing club's deserted.
Races were cancelled:
gale force wind.

She's immobile at the mooring,
turned stony by some damage
to her boat or self-respect
inflicted in the race, scratch race
they got up anyway,
a few of them.

The rest are at it still,
heeled horizontal,
hurled about by gusts,
their dinghies' washes latticing
the gale-wracked river.
To one of them she's lately married.

It was his plan: to sail
at the limit of the possible.
In it she's failed.
She sits alone, in straits,
after some stress
beyond her power to handle.

Pam Joll

I AM A WATER BABY

I am definitely a water baby,
That is plain for all to see.
With rubber ring and arm bands,
You surely know it's me.

I am the one that sits upon the side,
Just dipping in my toes.
The water is never warm enough,
And I can't bear it near my nose.

Eventually, I do get in.
Now that is quite a feat.
I stand there bobbing up and down.
This fear of water I shall beat.

I let go, and then I float.
Perhaps I could swim a while.
I think that might be possible,
If I try the breast stroke style.

The water is getting in my eyes.
My face is getting wetter,
But I really have to learn to swim,
And I'm sure I am getting better.

Yes! I am a water baby.
Today I proved it well.
I did three strokes across the pool.
And tomorrow, who can tell.

Jill Pettitt

WAVE

I am the pure wave,
from far out at sea
I come,
rushing, rushing,
to the shore.
Aquamarine and diamonds,
curved like a smile,
I summon my strength
through passive wiles.
I am the pure wave,
from far out at sea
I come,
rushing, rushing,
to the shore.

H R Burns

WATER SPORT

Into the closet, clothes off in hand,
Now's the time, to get off dry land.
On with the wet suit, it's a little too tight,
The best time to surf, is the start of daylight.
Grab hold of your board and start to run
Into the water it's really great fun.
Finding a wave, that will carry me through,
Along the ocean, so cool and blue.
The feeling inside, as I float on the sea,
There's no other place on earth I'd rather be.

Susan Hansen

GO WITH THE FLOW

The water looked inviting,
The temperature just right,
I thought to do some swimming
Would make slack muscles tight.

Jumped in with good intentions
Ten lengths at least, my goal,
So with determination
I pushed off doing the crawl.

But hardly having done two strokes
I ploughed into a wall
Of pensioners standing telling jokes,
It wasn't right at all.

I floundered round the laughing group
'So sorry - my fault', I lied,
Only to find another troop
Five, swimming side by side.

Their gossip, ripe and juicy,
No option but to listen
Thought it my moral duty
While queuing up to pass them.

Eventually I swam around
Those bobbing octogenarians
But once again I ran aground
On yet more jolly 'pedestrians'.

It took an hour to swim two lengths -
The moral of my tale,
Never try the swimming baths
On senior citizens' day.

(But oh! the day is coming soon
When I'll be 'young' enough to join the fun.)

Mary Todd

THE SWIMMING LESSON

At sixty-two I'm learning to swim
On second thoughts should have gone to the gym
Well here I am at my first lesson
One of a number for a weekly session
Creeping down the steps of the pool
Trying not to look like a fool
With knuckles white I clung to the side
In deep embarrassment I couldn't hide
The instructor said with a somewhat frown
Come along now you are not going to drown
We are going to learn to float today
Float! I said in great dismay
I tried and tried with all my might
My bottom half vanishing out of sight
Floundering there like a great white whale
Forever reaching for the safety rail
From the side of the pool the instructor shouted
Breast stroke next, then I was clouted
By somebody's arms flailing round my head
Oh how I wished I were home instead
Grabbing the rail coughing and spluttering
Hoping they didn't hear me muttering
Along with the rest I stood in line
Waiting now for the instructor's sign
The breast stroke once again we tried
My eyes were watching either side
No more was I going to take a bashing
Stood well back while they went thrashing
Perhaps one day I'll get the knack
Of floating gracefully on my back.

Janice Richer

BEN AND THE SEA

We had a lovely holiday by the sea,
there was beautiful sands and scenery.
On a day that was cloudless, sunny and hot.
Did he have a costume? No he did not.
So in his shorts he ran into the sea,
he was like a child again happy, free.
He swam and he swam out there on the brine,
he hadn't been in since the year sixty-nine.

Casting off nothing and as fast as can be,
you followed him into the clear, crystal sea.
It was so funny, you both made me laugh.
For you do a runner when we mention a bath.
I stood and I watched from the seashore.
Never knowing who was enjoying it more.
We'll never forget the time by the sea,
when you little Ben kept us company.

Marie Little

POND LIFE

There used to be fish in
                the res',
till the pit closed down.
Now it's filled in, not a
                fish to be found.
They belonged to the coal board,
so they took them away, as
                where they went,
                nobody would say.
There's no fishing, no more
                sparkling life,
so the bosses could win,
                now that's real pond life.

Rachel Oxtoby

SWIMMING

It seems there's no age limit when we first take to the water
A babe in arms is often there remembering all that gran has taught her
It's such a healthy pastime for the young and more mature
And for problems muscular it can help in some way with the cure
Of course there are those who will dash up and down
With back stroke and even butterfly they really go to town
They only pause a second to say how many lengths they've got to do
While we're just splashing round with some as experienced as you
We've even got time to socialise and pass the time of day
For us to attempt those twenty lengths there really is no way
We must admire the experts and we are a little envious
For the way they get those limbs to work with, it seems, so little fuss
They take part in many sponsored swims getting money for good causes
Some persevere despite their age dedicated for in that there are no pauses
The facility for swimming is there for all to share
The old, the young or the infirm, there'll be someone there to care
With even means to lower them down if they're unable to walk
For some can swim but need this help, they only have to talk
Years ago we did not have the use of local pools
But now swimming is within our reach and available to all schools
The encouragement to take part in this pastime is something to be commended
In fact from doctors it will almost always have been recommended
And so it's hoped that more will make up their mind and take the plunge
It's quite likely that it could extend their life if only they would indulge

Reg Morris

UNSYNCHRONISED SWIMMING

I'm bobbing about on the briny,
I've breast stroked a little as well.
I've dog-paddled, and I have floated
drifting nicely along on the swell!
When I first found myself in the water
I debated on giving a shout,
Then I thought about 'off-shore pollution',
you don't know *what's* floating about.
So pressing my lips tight together,
and lifting my chin out the brine;
I could feel my extremities cooling,
I could hardly believe they were mine!
There I was, having fun on the ferry
on a trip to that nice Isle of Wight;
throwing bread to the gulls, when I leant out too far,
and rapidly vanished from sight!
Now, it's not quite how I had expected
my outing to turn out to be;
And I wonder how long it will be till they guess
that the 'splash' that occurred had been me.
So, I'm bobbing around with a stiff upper lip,
(though the rest is all wrinkled and soft)
But hark, there's the sound of blades spinning round.
There's a 'copter a'whirring above.
. . . Now I'm wrapped up, and cosy, and happy.
This disaster is proving OK.
These rescue squad hunks have treated me fine,
it's turned out one heck of a day.
So the first thing I'll do when I leave the crew
is get on the phone pretty quick.
For I don't give a jot for the soaking I got,
I'm booking a trip for next week!

Rosemarie Varndell

WATER SPORTS

I'm on my holidays in June,
I'll take a plunge now on the flume,
Climb the ladder, to the top,
Lost my bottle now, but can't stop.
People behind won't let me down,
Right now folks then, hope I don't drown.
Down the shoot to the bottom,
Wicked people, how rotten.
Under the water, life flashing by,
Can't you see me, or hear me cry?
Someone help me, I'm gonna die.
As I gasp for my breath
Was this a vision of my death?
Hairy, scary, not for me,
I'll stick to sittin' by the sea.

Janet Elizabeth Isherwood

RAPID DESCENT

Blue boat, dark water
Slowly ahead, slowly breathing, heart slowly beating
Faint distant rumble, flickering white dancing horses
Rapid ahead, rapid breathing, heart rapidly beating
Blue boat, white water
Into its mouth, down its tongue
Spitting, frothing, kissing my face
Feel the force, harness the energy
Body twist, knees braced, mind focused
Cut, dive, slice, relentlessly onwards
Under the cold blanket, swirling darkness, eerie silence
Hip flick and up, dazzling sun, gasping for breath
The river submits, I am released, set free
Slowly ahead, heavy breathing, heart still beating
Blue boat, dark water

Andrew Livingstone

THE RELUCTANT SWIMMER

Well, I've eased into Lycra
(I try not to laugh)
I'm here to get fitter
At the local swimming bath.

So I jump in the water
(I wish I hadn't come)
But I can't leave before
Thirty lengths have been done.

As I begin to swim slowly
My technique starts to fail,
Splashing all around me;
Legs paddle, arms flail.

I'm no Sharron Davies
Or mermaid in the sea,
I just want to be fitter,
A thinner, healthier me.

Having struggled ten lengths
I call it a day,
This swimming's exhausting
There must be an easier way!

Genevieve Stone

A VERSE TO SURFING

I'm sorry to say, I'm in a bit of a plight
If I use my surfboard it always takes flight
Head over heels. I crash into the sand
And I must have twisted my hand.
I've swallowed the ocean - three times or more
I'm trying my best but my body's all sore.
Bruises in places I wouldn't show the old man
I really feel smashed, like an old tin can.

I'm taking a chance - am I being a bore?
Oh! But I think I'll try it - just once more.
Here comes the wave - I'm going to be brave
The waves gave a swish - help! I've swallowed a fish!
I'm going home, aw! What the heck!
There ain't no sense in breaking my neck!

Eileen-a-Lanna

SAILING THROUGH MARRIAGE

When I first saw my man's fine boat, I thought her wondrous beauty
Would draw me to a life afloat - first mate would be my duty.

He said that sailing would be fun. At first I thought it true.
But then a huge wave left me numb, and tension with us grew.

She is his love, his fair big boat. He talks to her each day
And all I do is lose his vote if I won't go and play.

The boat she tips from side to side, the loo is never still,
And getting wet I can't abide. I always catch a chill.

He photographs and looks at her, he loves her so to bits.
He never does such things to me. I think it is the pits.

He spends a lot of money, too, on making sure she's happy.
She's coiffed and tended, good as new. Meanwhile I'm feeling snappy.

He can't resist the strange desire to be at sea for hours.
The waves so big, forever higher, they give us constant showers.

He seems to like it. Really. Truly. He seems to think it's great.
And when the sea becomes unruly, his spirits just elate.

I know he loves his boat, I do, but why drag me along?
I've tried so hard to be the crew - for me it's just all wrong.

So sailing's fine when weather's fair, but England, we all know,
Is wet and cold and sun is rare and sailing I'll not go.

Patricia Yeowart

REBORN

Curled as a mushroom
bobbing beneath the unruffled surface
expelling the air,
bubbles rise around my foetal niche
I tip, turn and rotate
passing through a gate
of silence, safety and warmth
landing with a thud
before surfacing to draw
my first breath of air
greeted by the fumes of chlorine
splashes and bomb dives
of playful children
watched by anxious parents
as they splish, splash and splosh
in the now wavy pool.

Nicola Linfield

LOOKING ON

I am standing on the edge
Paddling in the salty sea
My costume is just too tight
it is the wrong colour for me
i wish that I could swim
The waves would be a shelter
I'd not need to be fashionably trim
And in the sun I would not swelter
I would swim out into the sea
And drift in with the tide
To be athletic is my plea
And not in a large towel hide

Glynis A Foster

WATER SPORTS MAESTRO

I really love all water sports
and try each different one,
but I'm clumsy, and I'm awkward,
and for me it's not much fun.

One day I watched a woman ski,
she zig-zagged through the waves,
so I tried it the next morning
feeling valiant and brave.

But I couldn't get it right,
the water came up to my knees,
and every time I started
I was swallowed by the seas.

So I thought I'd go surfboarding,
I *knew* I'd do that better,
but I forgot to take my shirt off
and my clothing just got wetter.

At swimming I am very good,
and I last for several lengths,
or I thought so 'til I started,
but I hadn't got the strength!

What else was there for me to do?
I pondered all day long.
Should I learn to drive a boat?
But I'm sure I'd do *that* wrong!

So I think I'll have to give up
all those sports of watery type.
I'll just lay back in a deckchair
and smoke my smelly old pipe!

Daphne Richards

YACHT RACE ON BOATING LAKE

The brink of a marathon,
Yachts with sails fluffed by the breeze,
Easy now, easy there's a long time to go,
And slow and steady a stately line,
Spreads out on the lakes clear surface,
The pace determined by a forewind,
That ruffles to a million tiny waves,
The water slate grey beneath a benign sky.

Circle of swans rudely scattered
By the lake invaders,
Edge the island in the middle,
As crews unriddle the problem of the bend,
For quickened speed and tossing dipping sail.
Skill needed not to capsize
And be a wader to the shore.
Success and the first round conquered,
Sail on round after round.
Till day gives way to murky dark,
And crews change throughout the night.

In the first morning light.
They make a brave sight.
Colours blue, white and white with pink.
Spread out on the lake's cold surface.
The race, an annual event,
Is almost spent.
And the judges' decision will be final.

Freda Grieve

SPORTING CHANCE

The sea looked so inviting
Sun was shining bright
Sand like golden sugar
Everything just right
Eyes on chunky lifeguard
Muscles rippling right
Fell over the deck chair
Blinded by the sight
Contact lenses disappeared
Couldn't see a thing
Helping hands led me away
(Was it my handsome king?)
Back on seashore, specs adorned
Looked for my shining knight
He was walking my best friend
Things were not swimming right
Desperate measures I behove
Swam out into the tide
Sank to the bottom like a stone
So mouth to mouth he plied
But it was not to be for me
False tooth went flying high
I'd given my 'eye-teeth' for him
And was still left high and dry . . .

Margarette L Damsell

VIRTUALLY SWIMMING

I wish they would bring in virtual swimming,
Then I wouldn't have to get undressed again
               at 8 am on Sundays,
And expose my far from perfect body
To people that I know.

Rosa Barbary

WATER BABY

I am a champion swimmer,
The best there's ever been.
My gold medal collection
The largest ever seen.

My sleekly muscled body
Makes men think I'm a dish.
I swiftly glide through water
Like some exotic fish.

My backstroke and my breaststroke
Are really quite supreme,
My butterfly and freestyle
Are every swimmer's dream . . .

But now I'll confess I'm a fibber.
My medals are nought but a dream.
I'm not such a wonderful swimmer,
A waterbabe I've never been.

I'll never get to the Olympics.
My chances of gold are remote.
So please help me blow up my water-wings,
And would someone pass me my float?

Angela Tomlinson

THE WAVE

I pierce the wave
My bow descends
The cold-melt river
Through valley wends

I surf the wave
And its my friend
To cross the flow
Its help it lends

I play the wave
And how much fun
It does provide
Run after run

I fear the wave
With this we must
Give much respect
But never trust.

Chris Leesmith

WHY DO THEY DO IT?

I settle down at the edge of the lake,
        The sun is comfortingly warm.
The water's as calm as a mill-pond -
        Then the *wet-suiters* have to perform!
Floating a board - neither raft nor a boat -
        Their feet firmly set into place
They struggle and tussle to bring up the sail,
        Good job this isn't a race!
'Hooray! Good for you! ' I mutter aloud
        As a blue sail is almost upright.
But, before this contraption can get under weigh,
        Its rider has sunk out of sight!
Splashing and dripping he surfaces again
        And clambers aboard it once more!
I guess that his aim, his ultimate goal,
        Is to conquer the furthermost shore.
After a while I fancy a stretch -
        We wander along as we talk.
We soon find ourselves on the other side -
        Why don't *they* get out and walk?

Beryl Jones

THE BIG SPLASH

To please the grandson whose name was Tim
Grandma thought she'd learn to swim
Then oh my! She did declare
I haven't got a thing to wear
So off she went into the town
Her brow all furrowed into a frown

To buy a costume one that fits
And covers all the extra bits
So she chose one 'twas very black
Which almost could have been a sack
The shop girl said that she should try it
How she wished she'd kept the diet

Off she went to the nearest pool
Feeling such a silly fool
When into the water she just crept
When mostly all the others leapt
And soon she swam just like a frog
Instead of paddling like a dog

Saying I'm happy that I learnt to swim
My figure's getting really trim
It makes me feel so fresh and good
And perhaps one day I really could
Try the highest board and dive
Then I'd know I've come alive.

Isobel Clanfield

SLIP UP IN SCUBA SCHOOL

A friend of mine was finally talked around,
to participate in a sport away from the ground.
So was it in water, or was it in the air?
It was scuba diving, what a dare.
She went out to sea on a great big boat,
nervous and worried with a lump in her throat.
I don't know what happened out there, she said 'It's a piece of cake,'
I still say she said that for all her friends' sake.
The funniest part was when she got back to shore
she wasn't diving, she fell on all fours.
She saw a graze and started to shout,
everyone wondered what it was all about.
Her dad went running, she'd slipped on seaweed.
her dad also managed to get tangled in the reeds.
They were both laid out in a heap on the shore
wishing they hadn't stepped a foot out the front door.

Louise Needham

MAKING A SPLASH

I went for a swim one Saturday night,
Dived in, stood up, and had quite a fright,
My costume had slipped and something fell out,
And I didn't want that spoilt brat to shout,
But he did, everyone saw, and I felt such a fool.
I popped it back in and just left the pool,
It was months before I went back to swim half a mile,
But the same pool attendant and boy what a smile,
He asked me my name and said something quite witty,
I won't say what he saw, but he said it was pretty.

Caroline Brankin

THE EDGE

Bitter cold memories,
Melt within the river of sadness.
A blanket of disbelief,
Falls over the world of canoeing,
Covering broken hearts with emptiness and despair.

The day was cold and wet.
Remembrance triggers,
An electrifying shiver up my spine,
Tripped out by the fear of repeat.
Rapids on the Afon Teifi roared,
Capturing Welsh canoeist within its challenge.

Daring paddlers paddled on,
Knowing not the consequence of searching
For *the edge* that is . . .
A borderline on which canoeists live or die,
Making adrenaline soar like a good day at Silverstone.

My blood disturbed by a siren,
Silence entrapped the noise with curiosity.
A vision of a rescue boat blasted hope,
The knot in my stomach belaying fear around my body.

We waited anxiously
Picking up the pieces of fallen hope
Ice melting against my cold, clammy skin.

'An accident, he wasn't going home again'
Harsh words of strangers
Drove spears of ice into our hearts.
Heavy tears crashed like waves on a windy day.

Kath Pigdon

THE DAY I BELLY-FLOPPED

With arms outstretched, up to the skies,
I walked the board to nervous sighs.
I arched my back and sprung with vigour,
Just like a bullet, released by the trigger.
I leapt, I flipped, I couldn't see,
I banged my eye with my left knee,
I entered hard and with a splash,
My reddening body proved I had hashed.
My diving days have all but stopped,
Since that day I belly-flopped.

Christopher A J Evans

SWIMMING MEMORIES

It was joy some years ago
Early mornings to the swimming
Pool I go
No matter what the weather
I would gather my things together

In the quiet such a treat
The water and the heat
Such bliss, no kids
Take a sauna
Take a shower
It was the most blissful hour

Kept my figure through my swim
Felt so fit, looked so trim
But those days now are so dim
When the kids left home for school
And I went down to the pool.

Antoinette Spooner

ANOTHER SWIM

Water conceals my body,
Lets me swim out into the sea,
I experience its docile touch
As it gently ensconces me.

My nose recognises the salty smell
That refreshes that familiar place in my mind,
Swimming helps me discover inner secrets
That I wouldn't usually find.

Waves delicately gurgle
And lap against a warm white beach,
My arms and legs plunge in time to the melody
That clings to my brain like a leech.

The water changes with my mood,
I become more inspired and alive,
It froths up into a mythical frenzy,
And I gaze in awe as the ripplets collide.

Fish lightly tickle my feet,
Searching for scraps of food,
I swim faster with outstretched limbs,
The water contributes to help me elude.

Right now nobody can hurt me,
I am protected by water and freedom,
When I glide in my vibrant swim,
I am in my own personal kingdom.

Sullenly I leave the water's sanctuary,
The dry land feels like a sin,
For now my dreams are forgotten and buried,
Until tomorrow when I'll go for *another swim*.

C M Vickers

DISAPPOINTMENT?

'Swimming class?' she calls - 'Let's go!'
'Can we go see Nellie?
I'm going to be a mermaid
Like the one on the telly.'

'Look at me Mummy!
Look at my fast legs'
As she kicks and kicks
Doing her *big arms*
Around and around.
'I can do it!
Will I get a Teddy Bear badge?'

Standing tall, they all jump in
Putting their heads under
No fear
Wet faces
Big smiles
As Nellie hands them the *pink slips*

Danni is scared
To wet her face
Not knowing
She cries
'I don't want to be a mermaid.
Can I go in the little puddle now?
And then have a drink and some chips?'
So we did
As the others all exchanged
Their *pink slips*.

Wendi Hudson

SLALOM AT APPLETREEWICK

Men standing rigid, a girl with blue knees,
Water is dripping and there's wind in the trees.
There are hundreds of boats where cows might chew cud,
And where all was once green is a quagmire of mud.
There are ribbons of brown on the field forming arrows,
Showing the way to the rapids and shallows.
A group of officials stand round in a ring,
Some holding wires and some *hairy string*.
The course is erected, the judges are briefed.
My number is missing. Who is the thief?
'Sorry! Old pal,' it's covered in mud.
All around, the spectators are thirsting for blood.
it's cold and it's wet and the sun dare not look.
A man with a 'tash lifts his head from his book.
A flurry of spray as a paddler goes by
Then the sun reappears from a cloud in the sky.
A flurry of spray as he passes by me.
The starter looks up from a mug of cold tea.
'Are you ready to go?' 'Are you *forty nine*?'
My number is loose but I've still got some time
To repair it.
I start to breath deeper, get my lungs full of air.
Club mates are watching - but why should they care?
My belly is wet from the very first wave.
I've just got a *ten* so ten seconds to save.
At the fall up ahead a paddler is swimming;
But the judge on the fall shouts 'Keep on coming.'
As I pass by, I steal a quick glance
At a boat bent in two. There isn't a chance
To repair it.
The finish sign looms up ahead.
Three gates to go and my arms feel like lead.

The whistle is blown as I cross the line
And drift to the bank. I'll recover - in time!
A cup of hot soup is thrust down in great haste,
And a glow from within brings a smile to my face.

Ken Langford

BORN TO DREAM

I skim the horizon on zephyr-like breezes,
We're king of the ocean, my sailboard and I.
I sail to the east and I speed to the west,
As exuberant seagulls go circling by.

The wind fills my sail, through the surf I go crashing,
Salt spray in my nostrils, the sea in my veins;
My respect for the waves is my only insurance,
I'm ever aware of the power of the main.

I was born to be free, yes my life is the ocean,
The water's my berth and the wind my pillow.
Such a buzz do I glean from this contact with nature,
As I whoop out a greeting to Neptune below.

Limbs twist and they turn as tired muscles are tested,
My board braves the swell of the silvery sea;
Blue, billowing sail keeps me journeying onward
As I plough through the deep, briny water with glee.

Then the wind changes course, I lose balance and flounder,
I'm dumped in the brine and I let out a scream;
I've turned over in bed and slipped onto the floor!
Yes, I know . . . well, we all have to dream our own dreams.

Kay Spurr

OPEN BOATING ABC

A   is for aluminium, awkward and aches.
B   is for birchbark, bruises, tea breaks.
C   is for C-stroke and Canadian of yore.
D   is for doubles, dunking and draw.
E   is for exit and empty it out.
F   is for figure-of-eight, flailing about.
G   is for goon, gunwale and 'Get me back, please!'
H   is for horrible, swollen-up knees.
I   is for Indian stroke and icy dip.
J   is for J-stroke, jump-out and jip.
K   is for knee pads for when we're not standing.
L   is for launching, leaning and landing.
M   is for macho men in a mood.
N   is for needing vast quantities of food.
O   is for obsession with Old Towns I might buy.
P   is for planking, plonking and pry.
Q   is for quiet and quick release knots.
R   is for rescues, and believe me, there's lots.
S   is for Star Tests (less said the better).
T   is for tumble-home, considerably wetter.
U   is for underwater and under-attaining.
V   is for very wet, soaked and still raining.
W   is for worthwhile, when all's said and done.
X   is in exhausting and in extra-fun.
Y   is for yawning and going to bed . . .
. . . you find something to go with Z!

Liz Beard

FROM CREEKS TO CRESTS

Strong and stable. Cockpit craft.
Single seat. Roamer's raft.
Transom *touring*. Timeless thrill.
Flighted fishers - statue still.

Dashing double, feathering fast.
Haslar hopefuls. Leading. Last.
Marathon mileage. Resisting rest.
Panting portage. Training's test.

Helmeted Hussar. Stencilled steed.
Buffeted balance. Sinuous speed.
Roaring rapids. *White*ned *water*.
Graded gradients. Fearful faulter.

Aching arms. Penalty poles.
Shipwreck stopper - requiring rolls.
Gauging gates. Reversing. Rough.
Slalom session. Tough on tough.

Compass checking. West-sou-west.
*Sea*man's sense in boatman's breast.
Lookout's 'Land-Ho!' Pin-point pride.
Caveman camping. Treacherous tide.

Rodeo riding ripping runs.
Polo pools. *Sprint*ing sons.
Daring daughters. Daunting dads.
Kayak kids. All mildly mad.

Peter R Lander

ODE TO THE JUNIOR SQUAD

Halloween '94 was a fateful night,
GB Junior Team Manager - what a fright!
Weekends to plan without a hitch,
Cancellations - no water, perhaps there's a ditch!
Letters and phone calls consulting with Pat
Trying to decide to do this or that!
Names to remember, goodies to take,
Pasta, fruit and Jeanette's fluid intake!
Physio Chris supports us through pain,
Shrinks Tara and Nicki help sort out our brain!
Another phone call and Teesside's not on,
Back up to Abbey, this time the water's not gone!
The level was great, the haystacks unique,
Sessions galore with lots of technique!
Oh dear, what was the norm?
Malc, Neil and Kev were all on top form!
Chris, Andy and Steve were not far behind
As coaches go, *brill*, six of a kind.
Mountains of food such as never before seen,
Janet and Alison, cooks, Haute Cuisine!
November to February lots of penalties about,
Selection is looming hope training's worked out!
We've come to the end, our aim is *the best*,
We've done our bit - you do the rest!

Chris Muir

SWIMMING

Racing, chasing and winning.
Mingling, tingling and grinning.
Empowering, showering and slimming.
These are the charms of swimming!

Paul Corrigan

A RELUCTANT WATER BABY

When I venture into the pool,
I am far from cool,
I run into the water, with haste,
Because around my waist
Is a large rubber ring.
- What's wrong with that,
I hear you say,
Well I was thirty seven the other day.

Dressed in black, slimming colour,
So they say,
It doesn't seem to be working today,
I can feel the flab fighting to get out,
Let's run in now, while no-one's about.
If someone splashes me,
I start to frown,
And shout 'Help, I'm going to drown.'
Without my glasses, I just can't see,
So I bump into people near me.

Once I was dragged onto a slide,
I was so scared, I thought I'd died.
For years my swimsuit never got wet,
Mention water and I'd be off like a jet.
Standing in the pool, wrinkled and pink,
With waterproof mascara, running when I blink.
I'm not going to visit the pool again,
if I want to get wet, I'll stand in the rain,
A reluctant water baby, that's me,
I'd rather be a *couch potato*,
At home on my settee.

Karen E Poad

THE FOOL IN THE POOL

I only came here to have a quick dip
And never intended my lunchtime *strip*
I've been in this pool since almost noon
Now my fingers and toes resemble a prune!

I shouldn't have tried out diving those hunks
My best swallow dive has cost me my trunks
I'd like to think they've sunk to the bottom
But hope to God those hunks haven't got 'em!

They're sort of stripy, blue and black . . .
Oh *you'll* know the ones, the elastic is slack!
I thought when I bought them they were a bit loose
But the assistant came up with a feeble excuse

'They'll shrink in the water!' she said with a grin
Now a man of my age shouldn't be taken in!
But not wanting to seem small and pathetic
I let her believe I was *big* and athletic

Now stuck in this pool in my birthday-suit
Suddenly that girl doesn't seem half so cute
Normally speaking . . . I wouldn't condemn her
But she's the reason for my present dilemma

Now it's almost closing time at the pool
I'm the only one left and feeling a fool
I've been seeking cover but all I could find
Was a pink rubber duck some kid left behind

The attendant is restless I hear him shout
'Come on now sir . . . it's time to come out!'
But I'm staying put, despite his harassment
Till I *find* my trunks and *lose* my embarrassment!

Brita Bevis

A FISHY ARMY

Indian Ocean warm and clear,
Where snorkelling is such fun,
Pretty fishes have a look
At the foreign ugly one.

Watched by the Sergeant Major
And with a trigger quite near,
A soldier attacks my face,
A sweeper is in my ear.

Dazzling colours all around,
The surgeon needs to rescue me,
Dizzily I swim away
From this army in the sea.

Muriel R Wrigley

THE WATER BABY

Float, float, float in the water;
Swim now, if you can!
You will dive and thrive in the water
When you are a man!
You will race with pace through the water,
If that is your wish;
You will slide and glide through the water,
Swimming like a fish!

Yan Parlan

THE END

Left alone,he had come to the end
of his tether.
Had a notion that he rather wanted,
Intended to end
This life.

'Nothing to it,' he'd heard, but
Just how to do it?
Had no gun with a bullet in, and
A very sharp kitchen knife
For butchery was ever so messy.

From his roof-garden,
Saw the triangular sunfish that dipped in
The crystal-clear, tropical ocean,
Arranged with precision
Below a sharp-edged, distant horizon.

It would be so easy
To set out confidently, beneath fluffy clouds
And swim out to them, in the great sea deeps
Where there was no island haven,
And continue to make
Varied, strong strokes for a long distance further
Until very tired, and supported no more
By conscious conscience,
Or laws of floatation.

David Daymond

FIRST DAY SWIMMER

Preparation required for you are going to get wet,
One large absorbent towel, but you will not need it yet
A bathing cap to clasp your hair and cover up your ears
Your plastic water goggles to keep back all the tears,
As you scan the bottom of the baths of steamy hydrochloride
Be careful of the slippery tiles, you cannot help but slide.

Before you even reach the point of going down the steps
Into the blue inviting scene - better check the depths
You are only three foot six - do not stand by the diving board
As you really cannot swim at all, you can really ill afford
To look as though you are in the queue to walk the plank,
To reach the brink - to dive straight off and then to sink!

No, better hold the gleaming rail and carefully slip down in
You can feel the warmth, just as in the bath - but what an awful din,
Masses of children, but not like you, they are water wise
They jump and scream, dive off the side, you'd better watch these guys
They will push you under the water, until you gasp and splutter,
The same ones who back in the street will push you in the gutter.

Ten minutes of this swimming lark you know you have had enough,
So wrap the towel around, pretend you're really tough.
All in good time a swimmer you will surely turn to be,
Have no fear of water, then I will take you to the sea.
Perhaps one day you will even want to swim the Channel
You won't always stand, teeth chattering and your shoulders all a quiver,
You may take up riding on the surf or be a great life saver.

Pamela Gibson

THE LESSON

With my hand comfortable in his,
We plodded slowly to the water's edge,
Enjoying the warm squidgy silt beneath our toes.
I, prideful of the new blue ring around my middle,
Together we stood, ankle deep in the salty sea.
'Come,' he said,
'Push, push, kick, kick, breathe, breathe.'
And I did - no longer fat and freckled me,
I was a mermaid, I could swim.

Patricia J Castle

DON'T FORGET YOUR ARM BANDS!

I like to go down to the lake
And sit upon my boat
I just hope that I don't fall off
'Cause I can't swim without a float

I really enjoy scuba
There's nothing like the reef
But don't catch your shorts on corals
The snag's beyond belief

I revel when I'm at the beach
And surfing on the swell
It's lucky that I'm so small
There's room for you as well!

And yes, I love to water ski
It really makes me merry
But here's a bit of my advice
Don't do it from a ferry!

Tim Gough

J B VESSEL

Sunday morning had arrived at last,
Our vessel slipped the ramp the sea was calm,
Fishing rods made at the ready,
Today would be fishing good fun.

J B's outboard raced his vessel out to sea,
I wave to fishermen upon the beach,
J B smiled with pearly white teeth,
At heavy breasted girls laying upon speed boats.

We anchored up three miles from shore,
Fish came in dozens,
Mackerel came in by the score,
We fished the tide until we were full,
Three hours had passed my fingers were sore.

Our fishing came abruptly to an end,
A ferry decided to join our fun,
J B threw his anchor line,
Oh no! His outboard wouldn't run.

This ferry just kept sailing on,
As it passed ten feet from our bow,
He blasted his horn,
J B waved then saluted,
Then our boat went down!

My life this day flashed before my eyes,
I couldn't believe but the papers saw,
A rescue helicopter flew us back to shore,
J B just laughed about his boat,
My sore fingers went around his throat!

James Stewart

THE EX DESCENT

The day of the great race arrived. The sky was blue and clear.
The air was fresh and crisp, filled with excitement and fear.

The Killarney guest house breakfast room was full to overflowing.
The chitter chatter and the small talk was non stop about canoeing.

Loaded up canoes on top. Wet suits on they were set.
Drove the 17 miles to the start, ready to get cold, tired and wet.

First off at the starter's pistol were capsize kings Kenny and Paul.
Breaking in and breaking out they were going to have a ball.

Slow but steady was the motto for Jerry, Kerry and Rob.
Pochahontas and her Indian braves had got 17 miles of hard slog.

Next were the kayaks set to go. Fiona, Steve, Mike and John.
Steaming off into the distance, overtaking everyone.

Unfortunately bad luck struck as it very often does.
Pochahontas and her Indian braves capsized just past the start.

The capsize kings were true to form. They came out in a stopper.
it was at the famous Cowley steps they came out and came a cropper.

The bank support was bloody useless, couldn't recognise who to applaud.
Shouting encouragement to everyone cold, lonely, fed up and bored.

Again Cowley steps got some more victims. Pochahontas and her
                                                    Indian braves.
The marshall ordered them out of the water. They were slow to finish
                                                    the race.

The bank support when needed. To pick the poor victims up.
Went to the car to find it had gone. The police had picked it up.

Everyone finished the race and Fiona won a cup.
Except for the Indian crew who really weren't having much luck.

The car had been impounded so they started the long walk back.
Picked up halfway to the finish and given a lot of flak . . .

The Ex descent for many was a very thrilling race. But for two of us it was awful.

Can we ever again show our face.

Next year Pochahontas will finish. The bank support will support. We will not be defeated. We will win and we will support . . .

(Written on behalf of the Compass Canoe Club, London).

Julie Playfoot

TAKING THE PLUNGE

I look at my swimsuit tucked away
And in my mind I think and say
I must make use of this again soon
I try it on but face is full of gloom
In days gone by it used to fit
But now I can hardly get into it
That's when I began to realise
I was in need of exercise
And wonder if I would look a fool
Going for a swim at our local pool
Am I brave enough to do that
Or will other swimmers think I am fat
Shall I wait and try to slim
No I decide to go for a swim
At the edge of the water what do I see
No-one at all is looking at me
All are swimming and so full of fun
So in I go to share this with everyone
When I get home what do I say
I'm sorry I hid my suit away
And a regular swimmer now I'll be
So now that's the sport enjoyed by me

Merril Morgan

GEMS TO SEEK

See all the treasures down below
as the under the water we do go.
Fishes swimming in colours bright
so precious is this wondrous sight.
The coral reef what paradise
so much to absorb with our eyes.
Limpets, whelks and oysters for pearls
mussels, sea-urchins for boys and girls.
Jellyfish, starfish, crabs to see
sea anemones floating so free.
All these sea creatures captivate
those who view these riches so great.
Rippling currents attention seek
blues, greens and greys a glimpse to sneak;
oranges, yellows, reds also
such brilliant shades - how they all glow.
Shells to value, rocks to keep
always remembered then take a peep.
Enchantment for many to share
diving safely, always take care.

Margaret Jackson

SWIMMING LESSON

Every week going from school
We paid a visit to the swimming pool.
Not a sport I liked, I must confess,
But had to go nevertheless.

The water looking quite cold,
Not for me! I'm not bold.
Clutching at the rails all around,
Must keep my feet firmly on the ground.

That was such a welcome shout,
When the teacher said, 'Everyone out.'
Back at school I felt quite sick,
To the toilet had to be quick.

Not a swimmer I guess you see,
From a fright that happened so early.
But I am sure I miss a lot,
By not going in the pool when the weather is hot.

Evelyn M Harding

WIND SURFING

I used to go wind surfing
in the river Plym,
it was so enjoyable
apart from falling in,
I went in all kinds of weather
it didn't bother me,
I'd get wet anyway
whatever the weather be,
it felt so good
skimming across the water,
there was room for everyone
however many were there,
going off course down the river
used to make me shiver,
thinking I'd end up in the open sea
and that would be the end of me,
but I'd eventually get back
to the sea shore,
have a rest and then go back for more.

Linda Casey

THE CHANNEL SWIMMER

The chill grey sea swirled at his feet,
Lapping higher with each splashing stride -
Into heaving depths devoid of heat,
As he sought the writhing serpent to ride;
The gauntlet's been thrown, there's nowhere to hide.

The mood of the serpent could change in a flash
From gentle quiescence to foam-frothing rage;
He must be prepared for the terrible lash
Of this capricious creature that ne'er knew a cage,
And whose demonic power no man could gauge.

The fight would be hard, he'd need to be strong
'Gainst this menacing beast in its lair,
He'd be feeling the fangs of the serpent ere long;
Head down arms-flailing, he uttered a prayer
That his suffering he would be able to bear.

For suffering there would be, of that he was sure
When he saw the beast rear and the black cloud-mass fall;
The tempestuous onslaught he'd have to endure,
But his fear was the voice of command that might call -
To give up the fight 'gainst this monster so cruel.

But they let him fight on, and the serpent he rode,
As it gnashed lashed and crashed, this mortal to quell.
He had fought a long day and the raw salt-wounds showed,
Had the beast drunk its fill? Who could tell?
His mentors sounded the last *three mile bell*.

With his strength fading fast he reached for the shore,
Vanquished, the beast 'neath him lay -
Pulsing shallow and weak, gone was the roar,
It had been beaten in battle today
By this mortal on his victorious way.

Peter Haines

CANOEING IS LIFE

Had we not pushed back the frontier,
there would be true adventure.
Had we not created plastic,
there would be true craftsmanship.
Had we not developed the canoe,
there would be something missing.

Chris Paton

HAVE NO FEAR

C anoeists we all are
A nd we have from afar
N o time like the present
O n with all the gear
E nter the water and have no fear

Cheryl McGowan (10)

HIPPOPOTO-ME

It's twenty years since I last went for a swim,
In those twenty years since, I'm not just as slim,
The weather was good, the water looked cool,
So, I took a chance and went into the pool.
I made a big splash, my spectators did laugh,
For there was a hippo sharing my bath.

Rhoda Glanville

SKI RIDE

It takes a lot of courage
To go out on water skis
To queue up with the jet set
And say 'Can I have a go please?'

A one-piece is essential
Although it's not so disarming
As a two-piece might become a one-piece
Which would be very alarming!

The instructors are so handsome
You try to look casual and bold
When underneath you're shaking
And hoping you can do as you're told!

Finding skis the right size
Then walking on the beach
Down to the water's edge
Is the first thing that they teach.

Then waiting for the boat's return
Sitting on the quay
You are thrown a handle
And instructed 'Hold tight and follow me.'

Off shoots the boat with vigour
You are jerked upon your feet
'Whoopee I'm up and skiing' -
Then you feel the sea under your seat!

The driver of the motor boat
Signals as best he may
While in this funny position
You are doomed to stay.

Until Ow! Glug! Glug! That is that
You have to be fished out and driven back.

Barbara Fosh

FIRST SWIM

Mum put me in the water
Inside a big building today
I heard her call it a swimming pool,
But all I did was play.

Mum let me splash about a lot,
And what a mess I made.
I'm going to try when I get home
With a glass of lemonade.

Mum bobbed me in and out,
As if she was having fun,
Not poor me I'd had enough,
And was feeling rather glum.

I know I thought unto myself,
I'll turn on a few tears,
It never fails without a doubt,
I've been doing it for years.

Dawn Lesley Owen

ADRENALINE RIDER

Some take the pleasure from the turf
I am one who preferred the surf,
Riding in on the Atlantic breakers
(Not for the faint-hearted or fakers).
Just as the waves start to boil
My board becomes my hydrofoil,
My body takes the surfer's stance
Trying not to lose that fine-tuned balance,
Powered by my unseen mistral
Riding adrenaline back to fistral.

Arfur Mo

THE SWIMMER

At two years old he had a bath
In which to splash and play.
He had a yellow rubber duck
To pass the time away.

At four he had a paddling pool
In summer, on the lawn.
He had a boat to float in it
Until the sails got torn.

At eight he went to swimming baths,
They thought he'd learn to swim,
He tried and tried without success
Until they chucked him in.

And then he found that swim he must
If he was not to drown
So paddling like a puppy dog
He floated up and down.

At sixteen he could do the crawl
And practice gave him speed
He joined the local swimming club
A *dedicated* breed.

At twenty five he raced, and won.
At swimming he excelled.
At fifty five he swam for fun
Until his ticker failed.

So now he has to sit and watch
Whilst others pant and strain,
Remembering his past success,
Remembering the pain!

Geoff Jeffries

SPLASH

Here at last
I burst through the door,
Hand the person money,
Then slip, slide down the slop into the changing rooms.

Rapidly throw off my clothes,
Whiz my costume on,
Race towards the lockers with my clothes screwed up in balls,
Then stuff them in a locker.

I take the key and scramble through the din,
And rush into the water,
Down the slope I go with the water growing deeper,
It's freezing cold and nippy as I plunge my shoulders under.

Swimming round the island,
With the current up against me,
Buffed and pushed around,
Now for the jacuzzi.

The bubbly, jubbly water,
The wonderful bouncing around,
Then down the slide with a big Yahoo,
I land at the bottom again.

And then for *real* excitement,
The flume is coming next,
Flying down the slope,
Suddenly you're soaking wet and lying in the water.

Back out of the water, dripping all around,
Find my locker,
Take my things,
Change, dry and go.

Hannah Wharton (11)

LEARNING TO SWIM

I think I can swim, or so I think
When in the water, I float or sink
I try to swim, but sink right down.
People are looking and started to frown.
What is she doing, I hear them say
But I keep trying day after day.
One day I'll do it, and I'll show them
That I can swim like the rest of them.

Sheena Probert

ANOTHER SHORE

Oh! softly waking I see the sun,
my pulse is beating, my heart, it yearns.
For over there, through the scudding sea mist run,
the blurred and further shore, there burns,
the fires of the darkened night time fun.

Among the dunes and on warm sand,
we had barbecued, binged, all in our prime.
We had scud the waves, surfboard's grandslam,
to be the best and fastly outshine,
all other surfing sails, across the brine.

This is our way, to say 'au revoir'
to our darling friend who is Australia bound.
The land of the sun, sand and rollers wide,
where breakers, sea and white surf abound.
To welcome those that ride the board.
We might meet later, who knows, a friendly, smiling,
                                        surfing horde.

Alan Noble

CHRIS'S DILEMMA

Paddling the North Esk having lots of fun
The day was dark and dingy no sign of the sun
Paddling through the stoppers, over standing waves
Henry, Bob, Chris and Roger . . . kayaking the craze
We shot a little rapid and broke out to play
'I'll stick my nose in this stopper' I heard Chris say

'Oops' says Chris what's this, it won't let me out
I wish it would hurry up and spit me out
Scull, scull, scull, bracing high and low
How long will it hold me? When will it let me go?

No one to help me they've paddles downstream
I wish I was home in bed and this was just a dream
But sure as hell it's real and I'm stuck in this hole
I suppose the next plan must be an Eskimo roll

Brr . . . the water's chilly, my roll will have to be rock steady
Two or three seconds more and I'll be in the eddy
Oh no . . . once more it's dragged me in . . . what can I do?
I'm thinking the inevitable and going for a swim

As we looked on from downstream Chris swam to the side
His little lump of green blob was still churning round and round
Where this stopper is? . . . Guess you'd all like to know
We'll spare Chris the embarrassment . . .
. . . but some day may let you know!

Bob Durnan

LIQUID GAMES

The day ahead . . .
Frantic fevered week behind,
Sleek boat and paddle welded to your limbs
Hungry for the buzz in tumbling torrent
The bubble and the thrash
You play the water's game, happy now.
Or longing satisfied so calm in lakes still water
That peace fathomed still water, idling the mind.
Boats bow slicing at the pool layered mist of morning
Smells hard and clean
Shared senses with heron, swan and reed,
Red ferned mountain mirrored on the glass you glide
And something snaps, something speaks inside,
Your soul tunes out, happy now,
Smiling once again.

Howard Riley

IN MY BOAT, I LONG

I tell how in my boat I always long
For waterfall, for stopper and for wave.
I'm told that fear and weary limbs are wrong
That leisure should be pleasant and be safe.
'It's not a proper way to play', I'm told
as people slur my sport with this sad stance:
That I'm not fit for pleasure; that I hold
A gambler's life-denying debt to chance.
But should we call this passioned struggle 'play'?
When stoppers grip me with the force of death,
I flex my living strength and float away
with beating heart and new delight in breath.
Through this dark 'play', my life grows rich and strong
And pleasant, easy, pastimes are proved wrong.

Mark Davidson

CANOEING AT SYMONDS YAT

We've been there before and we'll go there again,
It's fun, it's exciting, it's the Wye weekend,
The canoes are all loaded, the equipment all packed.
We jump in the minibus, it's off to the yat.
We're staying at Biblins all camped out in tents,
Dreaming of things we could do if we had the confidence.
We paddle upstream, and the fearless they go;
Straight into the white water, where they're bounced to and fro.
In the eddies some sit, contemplating the worst,
Then a bump from behind sends them in there nose first.
A few paddle strokes and you're off at a speed,
Straight down through the rapids, you've got a good lead.
A sweep on the left and you're turning around,
Back in an eddy safe and sound.
The rush of excitement has come to an end, canoeing is exciting,
That's why we'll do it again.

Rachel Walker

CANOEING

Damp mornings, cold kit,
Muddy banks, feet slip,
Freezing water, roll in it,
Canoeing? I love it!

P Griffin

SITTING ON THE BANK

Now I'm a novice paddler sitting in me
boat,
I like to paddle this way 'cos it means that I'm
afloat.

Now, I've learnt to paddle upstream and I've learnt to paddle
down,
I've learnt to paddle sweep strokes that turn me round and
round.

Now, I've learnt to paddle draw strokes and paddle with all
my might,
I've learnt to practice splash supports that help to keep me
upright.

Now, I know I don't much like it with my head dunked under
water,
I do it to practice escape drill 'cos I know I really
oughta.

Now, I'm a novice paddler and I'm sitting on the
bank,
I'm dripping wet and shivering but I must be really
frank.

Perhaps I'd better see a shrink perhaps my head has shrunk.
Perhaps I'd better have a shower that river really stunk.

John Milliner

THE RAPID

A paddle glints somewhere downstream
The sign that means I am the next to go.
I break-in hard with calculated lean.
Like a floating leaf am turned
and taken with the bobbing flow.
        The line is clear it bears towards the right.
Its path betrayed by surface dancing faces,
To a false horizon, falling out of sight
Relentless noisy waters forge
The sturdy banks and secret rocky places.
        'Paddle and relax' I say.
'Focus all wit upon the task at hand.'
Driving through chaotic cobra spray
Hard sweep, support then support again
Through watery ways, to many mortals banned.
        Now from a chute I check the line.
White vees hint at boulders all awash.
Bouncing through great standing waves sublime
Draw hard and lean then sweep.
The rapids power is ended with a gush.
        The leafy canopy all around;
The sloping banks where cattle quietly graze;
Twisted roots and boulders in the ground;
Trapped driftwood bleached and mossy fences
add wonder to these ever-moving ways.
        When at times there is a need to dream
of joys that life has on a soul bestowed,
Think on the beauty of a tumbling stream
where comrades smiled in dancing sunlight;
the heart raced hard; adrenaline flowed.

Ron Brown

MY BROTHER'S DIVING ADVENTURE OFF THE SOUTH COAST

It was the brightest sunniest day
No cloud disturbed the sky
The sea was still like stretched out silk
Not a single wave rolled by
They took the boat way out of reach
Of deckchaired bodies on the beach
And stopped a while to contemplate
Marine life in its natural state
Then down they went two at a time
Into the depths of the blue green brine
Into that peaceful other world
Where untold secrets are unfurled
Down and down and down they went
In rubber suited merriment
Down past the dazzling coral reef
Where pretty shells have shark-like teeth
Past moving clouds of rushing fish
And dancing shadows that you wish
Would tantalise and then entail
The playful flick of a siren's tail
But then in sunlight's golden rays
They saw and in turn were amazed
In spotlight was a wooden chest
And to open it became their quest
So back to base with box on board
They speculated on their hoard
But then some wording on a brass plate
Read 'Here lie the ashes of Emily Tate'
Her last request to her family
Was that she should be buried at sea
At once they turned the boat about
And this time took her farther out

Julia Wallis-Bradford

IN AT THE DEEP END

Being at school in the forties when the World War was at its height
We had to make do with austere provision as the authority budget was tight.
I suppose we were lucky to obtain what we did and to have the chance
                                                                to learn
For had we lived in a war-torn city there would have been more concern.
I attended the local grammar school where we were conscientiously taught
All the main academic subjects and we were not deprived of sport.
We had extensive playing fields, adjacent to the school,
But for all swimming tuition we relied on the town swimming pool.
The baths, as we all called them, were a mile and a half away
And, as there was no transport, there and back took half a day.
The swimming baths were ancient and the cubicles austere
So we always stood on duck-boards for verrucae were the fear.
A cavernous echo reverberated around the spacious hall
But it's the pungent smell of chlorine which mainly I recall.
As we entered the shimmering water it always seemed so cold
But to duck one's head was warming, if you dare to be so bold.
Even walking in the shallow end it felt just like slow motion
And non-swimmers would feel as insecure as if 't were the Atlantic Ocean.
Learning to swim from scratch seemed an obstacle so immense
For it was not just learning a skill, it was gaining confidence
To let oneself go. When one eventually learnt the technique
It provided access to all water sports, which most sporting types seek.
But, why was it that the cubicles were so dark and dour?
And when you returned to change it was your clothes on the wet floor?
Why did our fingers feel so numb, that it nearly made us cry,
So that our shirt buttons we couldn't fasten or our shoe laces tie?
Although I regard my schooldays as, in the main, convivial
My memories of the swimming baths must appear, to you, quite trivial
And that is a shame for, in truth, I was certainly taught a skill
Which allowed me to become a swimmer. A skill which is with me still.

John W Skepper

A DAY AT THE SEASIDE

A trip down to the seaside sounded such a good idea.
So me and my friend Josephine, her dog bringing up the rear
Set off for Southend-on-Sea searching for sunshine, pebbles and fun.
If only I'd known what would happen I don't think I would have gone.

We'd taken our bikinis, one airbed and two towels.
We both jumped in the water whilst the dog just sat and howled.
Our arms were flung up in the air as we wildly splashed each other.
Then my bikini top flew off and landed in the water.

The dog rushed in, retrieved it and hurtled off up the beach.
A polkadot bikini gripped tightly in its teeth.
Jo fell over in the water and very nearly drowned.
'Well serves you right for laughing!' I shouted as I frowned.

Regaining my composure and covering me bits
I made a dash for safety I really felt a twit.
With towel wrapped around me I went to the loos to dress
Leaving half the beach in stitches, the others not caring less.
So we wended homeward and a vow I made in my bedroom
It was the last time I'd go swimming without a full swimming costume.

Barbara Eyre

THE SURFER
(Dedicated to Peter, Julie, Thomas & Daniel Miles)

In the warmth of the sun
my surfboard I would ride
the blue of the ocean
with each turn of the tide

Like a ballet dancer
pirouetting afloat
dancing on the sea
to her musical notes

A crashing of orchestral waves
as I rode the ocean
Just myself and my board
man and sea in perfect motion

Respect to the sea
whose waves crash these shores
when I smell her salty perfume
I have to take to my board once more

James Jarvis

COLLECTING THE SUNDAY PAPER IN COWAL

Overhead, clouds were breaking,
Bestowing a glimmering light of optimism.
The raindrops' pizzicato would soon pass;
But they tricked me and embarked on a crescendo,
Beating down on my round, wide, black shield;
Dropping off each spoke's end point,
to add to the pavement's pot-hole pools
and slight, squirming streams.

A melody repeats itself in my mind.
What is it? I can't remember,
But it keeps in time with my pace.
Careful! - Wide rivulet at the kerb!
signals Amber, from the brain.
Thanks, amber. I'm past paddling in outsize puddles.
Watch out! - Tattered, slimy leaves. Avoid.
We need the Ambers of this life.

The unnamed melody then resumes, to the rhythmic,
squeaky-squelch accompaniment from the footwear.

Mhairi Dwight

FRIDAY STREET KITCHEN

The gently moving tinkling fountain
From the tap and not the mountain
In my garden giving pleasure
I dream my dream at my leisure
Of floating over lands afar
Without the sound of plane or car
The water flows out of the dish
Into the next, there are no fish
To swim about
In rivers and streams you'll find the trout
But I can dream my fishy tale
And make a catch as big as a whale
I waken feeling all at sea
To find it's nearly time for tea

Trish Birtill

A NON-SWIMMER WITH FRIENDS

The look on his face
A complete grimace
Of a smile not a trace
Just pure cowardice.

He won't jump in

We try to persuade
Our pleas he evades.
He cannot be swayed
He is afraid.

He'll never jump in.

He clings to the side.
He'd like to hide.
The damage to pride
Cannot be denied.

Too scared to jump in.

Rowena Shepherd

THE SWIMMING LESSON

We're all off down to the pool today
School holidays you see
It passes on some time for us
My four kids, my friend, and me
It takes an hour for the changing bout
Flow up their armbands, then pass out
Then a lengthy conversation on the issue of the figure
'Do I look fat? does my belly stick out?'
'Oh no I'm sure my bum's got bigger.'
We creep like SAS men towards the swimming pool
'Quick have a look if we know anyone'
So I can suck in my stomach and act really cool
The coast is clear no one to impress
Thank God for that no more distress
We submerge in the water our day has begun
The children are squealing all having fun
We've been on the waterslide hundreds of times
The backs of my legs are red raw
My mascara has run down my cheeks and my chin
My eyes look all puffy and sore
Then into the pool walks the man of my dreams
Panic washes over my face
On your marks get ready off we go
To the changing rooms I race

V C Ball

FLOATING

Watching you three
Floating on the sea
A frozen moment
Held in time to me
How vast the ocean
The heat of the sea
You three having fun . . .
Watching me
You three floating on the sea.

Suzy Messenger

LOVELY DAY FOR A SWIM

Exhilarating it was that day
As I made my way,
Creamy waves whipped stiff
Stormed the sea cliff
With their spray.

I stood, my back to the wall
And faced it all,
As it splashed and crashed then gnashed,
Thunderously smashed
Me to my fall.

Engulfed in a smothering swathe
Of murderous monstrous sea:
Its plaything tossed mercilessly -
Grand mockery of a bathe.

Gasping and spluttering, by chance
I crawled from the monster's grip
Bludgeoned, blood splattered and ripped
I gazed on its jubilant dance.

Prudence Bates

THINKING OVER MARY'S INVITATION

Me swimming! That's a laugh,
Would there be enough water in the bath? And
Can I get into my bathing gear?
Size fifty it is, well pretty near.
Curvaceous me should look quite slick.
'Course if curves were in the right places
It would fit
I've a mauve and black suit, it was
Marked down in a sale.
I wonder, will I look just like a whale?
Who cares anyway, it's for the exercise see,
Mary, my friend is coming with me.
The two of us is double blubber, a
Job to tell one from t'other.
I hope that Mary is my friend or
Will I get pushed in at the deep end.
Come on Eileen, it's all for the best
The proof of the pudding is in the test,
Will swimming help my aches and pains,
Or will I get water on the brain?
Well, whatever, I muse, come what may,
It will be a highlight in somebody's day.

Eileen Holt

PBK 20

I have a canoe
She's forty-two,
Her skirt is red
And her top is blue.
I go by myself,
But she's made for two.
I'm going out tomorrow,
D'you like to come too?

Idris Owen

IN AT THE DEEP END

I'm not a swimmer but I like a dip
When the weather's warm, I take a trip
To the local old-fashioned swimming pool
Where it's not too crowded, as a general rule.

Last Thursday week was such a day
My housework done, more or less I'd say.
I packed my bag with costume and hat
And a hairbrush so my hair would lie flat.

I boarded the bus and reached my stop
Near the swimming pool and the hardware shop.
I paid my fee and went to undress,
And planned to swim to relieve my stress.

After half an hour my stress had gone,
I went to dress and make my way home
I'd packed my bag with costume and hat
I'd brushed my hair to make it lie flat.
It wasn't 'til I walked through the door,
It must have been about quarter to four,
The bright gold chain from round my neck
Had gone! It must have fallen on the deck.

I rang the pool to see if it was there
The buses I asked if they knew where
My bright gold chain had chanced to fall
I knew not what to do at all.

I checked the pavement where I'd been
My treasured chain was nowhere to be seen
That night when I was about to undress
Oh dear, oh dear the return of my stress.

As I climbed into my bed,
On the pillow by my head,
There to my extreme delight
The gold it sparkled in the light
The chain was lost but now it's found
I'll sleep well now it's safe and sound.

Mary Johnson

LEARNING WITH PLAY

Becoming a member of the swimming
group, made me feel good it gave me
pleasure with plenty of thought for the
good of it
Lifting my arms across the water I began
to stride, isn't it leisure to
Glide with thoughts from the past.

Then a voice came from nowhere, 'What
are you doing, I thought you came
to learn, with the rest of us'. I felt
my face go red then, I replied 'Of course!
I came here to learn like many others,
That's why we are a group'.

Some have bands on their arms, why?
Fear they will drown? You won't drown
in that depth. Surprising, it's not the
first said Gillian, trying to unnerve
me at the same time. The coach spoke
to us about drowning, she's got a point.
I must learn this. We are all young
and I'm not considering the
younger ones.

Monica Rehill

THE DIVE

As he climbs the tension mounts.
This dive is the one that counts.
Climbs up high onto the board,
Then he dives with cool accord.
But oh dear! Alas and alack!
The poor man's elastic was too slack.
When he splashed into the deep,
His blue bathers he failed to keep.
Naked man to the side then rushes
Made haste to spare everyone's blushes.
Wrapped himself with a handy towel,
Onlookers with much laughter howl.

Josie Minton

LULLABY

Float, float, float.
Be the foam on the tidal wave.
Don't be afraid. Stretch your arms and legs.
Float, float, float
On the tidal wave between the sea and the sky.
Enjoy to be cradled to infinity.
If the sun blinds you, shut your eyes.
Lullaby of the sun, of the sky, of the sea
Sung for any woman for any man
In whom love abides.
Love rocks you to eternity and flies high.
Lullaby, lullaby, lullaby.

Angela Matheson

OCEAN ADVENTURE

It is cold, and it is windy, and waves thrash at our tiny boat
Wind throws sprays of water at me, and I hope we keep afloat
It's hard to walk in these flippers, and the oxygen tank weighs on my back
In this suit I feel so funny, trimmed with orange and mostly black
Now I brave the icy waters, sending bubbles all around
This is my first time at deep diving, now I wish for solid ground
But now I'm here, well I'm committed, can't turn back now, must go on
Then I hear another splash, and look to see my friend named Don
Don gives a signal, and I follow, we both descend towards ocean bed
The I notice all the sea life, fish of blue, yellow and red
Suddenly I feel excited, this is fun and not so bad
And it's calm down in the waters, and suddenly I feel real glad
It's not as cold as I imagined, in fact it was colder in the air
Now we reach the ocean floor with creatures beautiful and rare
It's like we are in another world, the richness of this unspoilt place
I see clearly my Creator's hand, and thank Him for His wondrous grace
Corals of unimagined splendour, for over an hour we explore
Creatures I did not know existed, and I just keep seeing more
But suddenly Don is pointing, and up above us to my dread
A huge shark darts through the waters, and suddenly the water's red
The shark has taken a large fish, and feeds with fury and with zeal
Is this all really happening, but somehow I just know it's real
I recognise Don's sudden signal, he wants us out of the water quick
I see the urgency in his eyes, and suddenly I feel real sick
Quickly we surface, and climb in our tiny boat, and not with
                                                                        a moment to spare
Suddenly the water is alive, and all I can do is stare
The blood has attracted a feeding frenzy, of sharks all sizes snapping mad
Don quickly starts our tiny boat, and we head towards shore, and I am glad
Well I've had quite an adventure, and Don suggests we go again
'Only if it's a no shark zone' I answer, and yell it out to make it plain.

Marlene Peckham

LAYING-UP

The golden days of summer are gone now,
gone with the boats into the shed.
The green of spring and the russet and grey of autumn
all dead.

The sparkle and splash of the water,
the joy of the fresh breeze,
gone with the boats into the shed.
The tug of the sheets and the pull of the tiller
fled.

The rudder a dead thing on the shelf,
the sails folded and supine,
all dead.

Frost closes down on the living water
and the weight of years lies heavy upon you,
the golden days
all dead.

Will they return? Will the boats
waken again to life,
proudly riding the new-born water,
dancing to the wind and the will of the helmsman?
Surely they will.

But who -
who will take tiller and sheet in his hands?
Will it be you?
Or will they say, as the fleet tacks up to the start,
'Pity he's dead'.

Peter Fenwick

ODE TO A WINDSURFER

Wind weaver, wave walker,
Elemental man, ocean stalker,
Sweet sting of salted spray,
Escape from yourself just hold it all at bay.

Rhythm of life along the sail it beats,
Body and ocean in spirit you meet,
When all becomes nothing, just the endless blue,
Wouldn't be hard to forget that it was even you.

Burdens of life can't reach you there,
Cast it all aside become the wind, without care,
Crashing into the deep, taste its freedom,
There's no pain out there I wonder, do we need them.

All those things that make us hurt,
Life under foot is so stagnant, almost inert,
When we could just be there dancing the surf,
So shackled and chained our like upon turf.

The breath of God it's just in the breeze,
Board and sails the altar, you worship with ease,
Is there ever a moment that you could feel more pure,
Waves under foot back turned to the shore.

That light in your eyes speaks of liberty,
Melody of man and wind then you are truly free.

Jemima Norman

SYNCHRONISED SWIMMING

Synchronised swimming
our group the over fifties
we thought it was a hoot.

It wasn't easy it was some fun,
floundering and splashing, giggling
and laughing.

Our efforts didn't go unnoticed for
a few younger ladies, join in with
our group.
To teach us how it should be done!

Then at last, it all clicked, we floated
right way up, with our arms intertwined
with toes pointing in the air, a formation of
a lily we made.

Synchronised swimming champion
we won't be, we will be the over
fifties group having fun!

Esther Rehill

THE DIVER

Flying through the air spirit's free,
The highest board,
The deepest sea.
Poised above the shimmering blue,
The diver dives,
His dreams come true.
Entering the water a perfect splash,
He surfaces triumphant,
A medal at last.

Elizabeth Camp

IN THE POOL

I saw you in the swimming pool
And recognised you straight away,
Despite the fact that you've grown fat
And your hair is going grey.

There were two children, quite grown up,
Aged perhaps twelve or thirteen.
Both of them looked just like you . . .
Or me . . . or maybe in between?

If you looked, you didn't know me.
I was slightly underdressed
Since last we met, and bald as well;
So if you looked you never guessed.

Never guessed that while our children
Swam and shouted in the pool,
I remained among the learners,
Hid my face and felt a fool.

Geoff Skellon

SURFING

As I surf upon the sea
There is no better place to be
I feel the waves caress my soul
I'm on a high, the waters roll
The sun is gleaming
The wind is warm
I'm on my way it's far from calm
Surfing high, surfing low
What a perfect sport to know.

Caroline Robinson

CRYSTAL WATERS

Dive into the waters clear,
The sounds below are all you'll hear,
See the world you don't yet know,
For this is where the oceans flow,
Feel the freshness on your face,
Feel your body glide with grace,
Swim into the crystal blue,
The temperature is nice and cool,
Vast amounts of rushing waves,
Lie in wait for sun-drenched days,
Come they call, we're here to please,
Experience our twinkling seas,
For here it's peaceful and sublime,
What better way to spend your time!

Carolyn Finch

OH TO BE IN THE WATER

Diver Dan and Seahunt were to blame
For sub-aqua diving being my aim
So when I was asked to 'suck it and see'
A try dive Christmas present was for me
After, I was all set to do the novice course
Only one thing left to be endorsed
A medical certificate to say I was fit
Then I could save up and buy all my kit
Only anaemia left me unable to try
To see if I really was cut out to dive
Now as the membership secretary of the club
I can see others learn and there is the rub
Because of these very strict rules
I can only watch from the side of the pool.

Melanie Burgess

A QUICK FALL IN THE SWIMMING POOL

When I first learned to swim
The teacher pushed me straight in

She wouldn't let me out
even though I did scream and shout

I begged my mum not to send me again
And explained that the teacher was clearly insane

Nevertheless she sent me once more
And as I opened the changing room door,

The teacher was standing there 6ft tall
And built stronger than a big brick wall

She took me through to the swimming pool
I thought my god this is worse than school!

I was in the water half dead,
when a thought popped into my head

It was a brainwave, an excellent idea
But I'd have to wait until the teacher came near

I called 'Miss, Miss quick
I think I'm going to be violently sick!'

I waited until she was stood on the ledge
And made sure that her feet were right on the edge

Then I caught her off her guard
I grabbed her heels and pulled hard

She fell in with a shout
And it took four lifeguards to pull her out!

She looked like something the cat had dragged in
And do you know what, she never could swim!

Gemma Daniel

COWES WEEK

Mid morning and the band play
This will be a great day
As the crowds mill about
In the sun children's ices melt
The people come to see a week of races
As the yachts are put through their paces.
The Solent becomes a sea of multi-coloured sails
Then the klaxon wails.
Competitors tack for their place
The canonn's blast starts the race.
As the yachts sail away
The crowds wonder who will win the day.
A stiff breeze helps the boats move with ease
As the Red Funnel ferry leaves.
Offshore the Royal Yacht Britannia is moored
I wonder if the Queen's on board?

Trevor Read

YOUNG AT HEART

I am an Aquarian by birth
In January I arrived on earth
The water-carrier is the sign for me
And my natural home is by the sea

On holidays I spend my time
Swimming in the foaming brine
No matter what the weather be
A dip in the sea is right for me

On any sunny summer's day
I'll join the children as they play
Paddling with a wooden boat
Helping to keep the sails afloat

If the sea is calm and the sky is blue
To me it's just a dream come true
A happy water babe that's me
Although I'm almost seventy-three

Ethel Hatfield

WATER PHOBIA

Water has always terrified me,
whether river, lake or tempting sea.
Surfing in Cornwall was a disaster
the sea of course was supreme master.
When the family bought a cabin cruiser,
we knew it was bound to be a loser,
the tide went out and left us stranded
it was only a sandbank where we landed.
A trip on the Thames was more of a joke,
the swans came too close and gave us a soak.
Navigating the locks was very precarious
and when I fell in they thought it hilarious.
A gale force nine in the Bay of Biscay
did not seem at the time to be very risky.
The ferry to Sweden was much more a treat,
enjoyed in comfort not such a feat,
and when we go to our local baths
friends deliberately stand and laugh.
I only swim for half a length,
somehow I never have the strength,
when the children are away at school,
sometimes I prefer to use their pool.
Terra firma is much more me
for a water babe I'll never be.

Barbara Harrison

WINTER SWIMMING

I like the notion of a dip in the ocean
On a hot sunny day in July
But when there's no sun, I say it's no fun
And I wouldn't say that's any lie.

I dislike hardy folk who think it's a joke
To dive into the Brighton sea
On Christmas Day, though like it they may
It would thoroughly frighten me.

Comfort and ease would better me please
Than a shivering time in the sea
A cold in the head and goose pimples I dread
And most people I think would agree.

And when you come out, there's a cold wind about
That makes the whole body shiver
And until you are dressed you won't feel your best
With a possible chill on the liver.

If the day isn't sunny, it's really not funny
To strip down and make for the beach,
I'd prefer a hot toddy to exposing my body
And keep a big fire within reach.

So let those who want, their blue bodies flaunt
And if necessary, break through the ice,
To drop 60 degrees would make my blood freeze
And that to me doesn't sound very nice.

William M Jones

SUN, SEA AND SEWAGE

All sails are set and with tiller in hand,
in soft summer's breeze, I stand off the land,
the clear green water sparkles bright in the sun,
a great day for sailing, a great day for fun.

The breeze freshens quickly, sails pulling hard,
I'm smart to the gunnel, I'm always on guard,
I luff up to windward, we gather more speed,
the white water foaming, streams past my feet.

The bright noonday sun burns hot on my back,
the land's far away, now I must tack,
disaster strikes swiftly, a net snags my keel,
taken aback by the wind, and over we heel.

Capsized in a tide race and I'm swept away,
has someone seen me? I hope and I pray,
my life-jacket supports me, I drift with the tide,
I study my companions, which float by my side.

There's bottles and beakers and bits of old rope,
take away cartons, and cans that held Coke,
syringes with needles and sewage join the stream,
I worry about e.coli, and hazards unseen.

No need for to panic, rescue is not far away,
an inshore lifeboat is skimming the bay,
cold and shaking, I'm hauled quickly on board,
then wrapped in a blanket, I'm speeding for shore.

And now as I lie, safe in my hospital bed,
I ponder on what the doctor has said,
'You swallowed much water, I'm sorry to say,
you've contracted hepatitis, we think it's type A'.

Affrug

WATERSPORT

As time goes by I feel the need
To prove I'm not so old,
But ideas that come into my mind
I feel are much too bold.
I thought I'd try to water ski
But found it really wasn't me.
High diving isn't quite the thing
To climb the board makes my ears ring.
I tried to synchronise my strokes,
But got mixed up with all the blokes.
Now don't give up I told myself
Exercise is good for health,
There must be something I can do
To keep myself as good as new!

Iris Selly

THE FIRST SWIMMING LESSON

He sat on the seats overlooking the pool
An uncertain look on his round baby face
I stood in the gallery, outwardly cool
Yet feeling my heart as it raced.

I wanted to wrap him up and hold him
Reassure him that things were all right.
'Just listen to the instructor', I told him,
When he asked about swimming last night.
Next thing I knew he was in the water, jumping and splashing around
Not a care in the world as he talked and played,
With a dozen new friends he had found.

In no time at all he was out of the pool,
His first big step had been taken.
This nerve-racking experience had taken its toll,
And I was the one who'd been shaken.

Paul Perry

FIGHTING THE FLAB

It was a boring day, with nothing to do
My best friend was ill, she'd caught the 'flu
So I then decided, it was time to get fit
But first I needed, to buy a kit.

So shopping I went, for sportswear galore
And ended up buying, most of the store
It was important I thought, to look the part
I hadn't done much, but at least it was a start.

Tennis was the sport, that I tried first
I can safely say, it was my worst
Hitting a ball, is harder than you think
So I thought I'd try swimming, and prayed I wouldn't sink.

I used to hate water, but realised I was wrong
And soon found my talent, and not before long
I could swim and dive, and splash a lot too
It's a good job my friend, had caught the 'flu.

As now I am fit, no flab in sight
I can wear short skirts and anything tight
I receive roses daily, and am asked out on dates
I am now the envy, of all my mates.

Shabnam Walji

CHAQU'UN

We're all off on holiday, south coast of Spain,
Have you been before? Oh, again and again!
We love it, the water, it's so warm and clear,
We can't help returning there, year after year!

The water? The water? But what about fun?
So don't you go there for the warmth of the sun?
And don't you enjoy all the food and the wine?
Relax on the beach when the weather is fine?

Oh, goodness me no, we just couldn't do that,
Just lazing around getting sunburnt and fat,
We love going whale-watching, far out to sea,
Or catching fresh mackerel, straight from the quay.

We're down at the pool every morning at seven,
With scuba tuition arranged for eleven,
An hour or two's snorkelling takes us till three,
With luck we can parasail just before tea.

We're first off the diving board, first on the sand,
First on the surfboards - you must understand
If water's involved, we just love to get wet,
But haven't tried synchronised swimming - as yet!

But wait! I'm a water fanatic, like you,
But Radox is what makes my water turn blue,
I've no room to swim, or to surf or to row,
My pool fits me neatly, from bath-hat to toe.

With space for my ducks to go paddling by,
As there in my bubbles, relaxing I lie,
I sip from my luxury glass of champagne
And drink to your health on the south coast of Spain!

Sue Holtom

SPLASHING AROUND I NEARLY DROWNED

Behind a boat attached by a rope in a freezing Cornish sea,
A stupid place to be you say, well yes I must agree.
So I'll start from the beginning, let this story just unfold,
How I got in this predicament I think you must be told.
I blame the wife, it was not my fault, I did not wish to go,
But once she makes her mind up then it's pointless saying no,
So to the beach she dragged me, it was something well worth seeing,
She handed this man money and announced we're water skiing.
You jest I said and smiled at her with a really sheepish grin,
You know my dear I'm sure you do that I cannot really swim.
But before I knew it in a wet suit I was clad,
The wet suit this was way too small and made me feel quite bad.
So finally we're out at sea by now there's no escape for me,
You know now how I got to be behind that boat in the Cornish sea,
You might think that's the story told but not quite I'm afraid,
I had to give this thing a try for money had been paid,
The boat took off with me attached I clung on what a blunder,
For my skis had both snapped off therefore I was dragged under.
You know a water skiing champ I never will be crowned,
For if I ever go again I'm sure I will be drowned.

Russell Pengelly

WAVE MACHINE

They've just turned the wave machine on,
There were loads of little kids in there but now there's none.
My friend went and tripped,
And my mom's swimsuit has just ripped.
They get out
But I stay in,
And all over my face there is a grin.

Victoria Clark (10)

LANDLUBBER BOOBY

Water babe I was never meant to be,
      Yet I learned to swim,eventually.
My fear of water I had to conquer,
      Should have done it when I was much younger.
With inflated rings on my upper arms,
      In junior school baths I'd come to no harm.
The water was only up to my waist,
      But I was no swan when it came to grace.

As the lessons progressed, fear receded,
      Until I sunk, then advice unheeded,
I flailed my arms, and took in water,
      Thought, *I'm drowning,* prepare for hereafter.
Surprise, surprise, I was upright again,
      No one had noticed, dignity remained.

Many were the fights I fought with water,
      I won through, like a swimming warrior.
Sense of humour, and determination,
      Brought results beyond my expectation.
I gave no credit to the instructor,
      She would have left me to drown, the monster.
That's not fair, she knew what she was doing,
      She knew how to turn this frightened being,
A scared of water, landlubber booby,
      Into a free swimming, water baby.

Marjorie Spark

THE SWIMMER

A key, a pen, a comb -
there in my pocket
this morning when I left home.
I didn't have to hurry,
I didn't have to dash -
but in a flurry I got to the pool
and made a big splash!

The water was warm
and everything shone.
But here! I came up
from the bottom
without my flippin' shorts on!
Luckily no one was watchin'
so I pulled 'em up
and started swimmin'.

The breast stroke is my stroke -
the deep end is my end.
But when it's crowded
it's difficult sometimes
to swim a length.
I go round in circles then -
in and around them all
until I'm out of breath!

A key, a pen, a comb;
there in my pocket
when I get dressed and go home
I don't have to pay
to use the pool
because my wife works here
and she's nobody's fool!

Kenny McPhee

COME ON GRANDAD

'Come on Grandad, you can do it.'
Cried the child with glee
Struggling not to show my fright
There was an old fool like me.

Swimming exercise is what you need
The doctor would oft-times preach
I listened as my grandchildren
Searched for someone who would teach.

Every week as lessons passed
Their prowess they dictated
As better they got, and stories they told
This fear I so much hated.

Protection was their parents' aim
Rules made when they were babes
Encouraging them to make a game
Of water sports, sea and waves.

'Come on Grandad, you can do it.'
A child's voice encouraging me
It's not far across the pool
'Come on - swim to me.'

Mary Williams

SPORTING CHALLENGE

I'm not a sporting person
But swimming I don't mind
I never enter races
Cause I'm always left behind.

People have their special ways
Of swimming to and fro
My way is the best way
It's the only one I know.

I do doggy paddle
No don't you smile
I swim across the baths
It takes me quite a while.

One day I will upgrade myself
And try a different stroke
Then people will take me serious
Instead of just a joke.

Patricia Belfield

WAVE POWER

Who dares take the wave
With all its power?
Who dares not take the wave
And be branded a coward?
Swimming out
On a stiffened board
That comes alive
When the wave roars.
Feel its power,
The mountainous surge,
As it lifts you up
And you get the urge.
Along a tunnel
Of ice-blue glass,
You emerge victorious
You've shown your class.
Today you've won,
You've done just fine,
But the surf may claim
The right next time.

Moira Brabender

ESCAPE

The pressure of the water
The shadows of the sea
Closed inside a space like world
Of special things I see

The colours bright and vivid
Old ships with tales to tell
Another world a secret place
With treasures hidden well

Without outside intrusion
Of normal worldly life
Away from all the clammerings
The worry and the strife

Complete peace and tranquillity
Just floating, being free
There never could be anything
But a diver's life for me.

Marie Hodgman

MESSING ABOUT

Messin' about on the river,
    Water seeps into the boat
And into the rug and the towel
    Then into my nice new coat.
My shoes are really sodden
    The picnic box is wet
The sandwiches are soaked and limp
    The biscuits? - Best forget!
But still there is a cup of tea
    And some milk in a tin,
Oh no! You must be joking . . .
    The river - the flask fell in!

Margaret Carter

SCHOOL DIVING COMPETITION

The teacher said have a go
Enter the school diving show
Forced into this tight spot
I said diving was not my lot
To say no was too late
Spring from the boards is my fate
Ready to climb to my spot,
Now it's getting hot
Fly with grace through the air
Will I crumble and belly-flop there?
No eleven it's time to go.
I feel the boards with my toes
My legs shake, my stomach turns
My bottle goes, I show concern
Can't back out must have a go
Continue on with the show
I'm at the top, up a height
Too high for me, what a fright
Ready for my final leap
Into the unknown and the deep
I push away and fly with style
It only lasts a little while
People gasp, what a shock
A giant belly-flop.
Too embarrassed to rise and look
Under the water I daren't come up
To the edge - still alive
Gallons of water swallowed inside
I look for a result on the wall
Strange no result at all!

Sean Flanagan

AGE IS NO BARRIER

As boy, at baths, I felt a mug:
all I could do well was glug!
Annoying water in each ear
often took some days to clear.

I gave it up! Became a man;
thought about a novel plan -
swimming lessons! Just one - 'twas grim:
pupils cried: 'Look! Sir can't swim!'

I gave it up! A friend said: 'But -
dinnertimes our baths are shut,
and I'm in charge, so don't be dim,
let me teach you how to swim.'

I did! I learnt! And had great fun!
Swimming styles: I used each one.
A hundred lengths in dinner hour
soon became within my power.

Life-saving called where learning soared -
gaining next-to-top award!
Now here it comes, the telling line:
I swam first at thirty-nine!

If your great fear is 'watered-ear',
punch sideways down - it will clear.
But join a club (for you're no mug)
Don't mind age. Do more than glug!

Tony Hughes-Southwart

WATERSPORTS

I do a bit of swimming,
Jacuzzi I love too,
The sauna afterwards as well,
Twice a week, I do,
My friend is mostly with me,
And we meet others there,
Losing weight we're aiming for,
Those sticky buns beware,
Or what we've burned in calories,
With all our hard work now,
Is wasted with a big iced bun,
Please don't ask me how,
I think we kid ourselves along,
Pretending we do well,
Then eat a thousand calories,
I don't think I should tell,
But never mind, we do have fun,
A kind of fun of sorts,
Jacuzzi, sauna, swimming,
Are my favourite 'watersports'.

Janette Campbell

I HAVE A DOG

I have a dog, his name is Mister
He likes to swim with me and my sister
But he doesn't like armbands, he thinks they're too tight
And neither does he like swimming at night
But point him at the Channel, on a nice summer's day
He rushes in, swims 20 yards and barks
Oh yeh man, see you in Calais.

Peter Hassall

ODE TO A BANANA BOAT

I'm easily persuaded, I can see that now,
A summer in Spain; survived; I don't know how,
Against my better judgement, I said 'Yes I will',
Five minutes of agony spent on 'Banana Boat' hell,
I was thrown to the left then tossed to the right,
I clung on so hard; I feared for my life,
Screams of delight and cries of 'Go faster',
The speedboat obliged and slammed round the corner,
We were all thrown off and half drowned in the water,
As we waited for the boat to take us back over,
I hope there's no sharks I spluttered to my friends,
'Plenty', they laughed, 'we are in the Med,'
The boat picked us up and took us to shore,
I examined my bruises now purple and sore,
My legs were all jelly, as I looked back out to sea,
Checking for sharks, which could have had me for tea,
Tomorrow, giggled my friends, we'll have a go then as well,
But I might not be so lucky next time, on banana boat hell,
Not me I smiled I had just survived it *this* time,
No way Jòse *am* I going back on, never ever again!

Tracey Thomson

NOT SWIMMING - DROWNING

I remember it well,
My friend said, 'Let's swim',
A race to the faraway bank,
The current was hell,
I floundered within,
He considered my actions a prank.

My arms turned to lead,
My mouth tried to shout,
But the water entered my cold frame,
I walked with the dead,
Before dog-paddling out,
Denying the reaper his claim.

Thomas A Rattray

ODE TO DIANA

I'm learning to swim, like I've always yearned,
Being scared of the water, I never learned.
And so I said, when I retire,
The first thing to do, is achieve my desire.

I'll conquer my fear, of my face in the water,
And of breathing in, when I shouldn't oughter.
Of jumping in fearlessly, at the deep end, to date,
Coming up with a gasp, then swim off, at a rate.

First, with the breast stroke, and then with the crawl,
I've even dived from the side, I'm learning them all.
By no means, am I perfect, but I'm working on it,
Our teacher's a slave driver, and we all do our bit.

Tuck in your chin, and remember to breathe,
A long stretch of the body, and just glide with ease.
Swimming should be restful, just lie back and float,
Be a little more graceful, she's great, she can gloat.

She sure keeps us moving, from my hips, I've lost pounds,
But at last, I can swim, no more fears of being drowned.
So, here's to our instructor, with pleasure, raise glasses,
May we all come through smiling, as Diana, gives passes.

Katherine A Ford

BOATING

The day my husband said to me, I think we'll buy a boat,
Little did I realise what life was like afloat,
I'd sat by the river, and watched the happy boaters passing by,
But thinking boating was sheer pleasure, well that was pie in the sky.

So only being amateurs, we bought a little boat,
Lowered it into the river, and once it was afloat,
My husband climbed aboard it, but underneath the water were boulders
                                                                                       we couldn't see,
So his weight tipped up the boat, and he fell out on his knee.

Then we got the hang of it and bought a nice speedboat,
Happily we enjoyed it, life was great afloat,
But one sunny afternoon, everything OK
Then my husband's cuff got caught in the gears, a nightmare of a day.

There we were in the middle of the river, engine had cut out,
But would you just believe it, no other boat about,
We reached the bank with out little paddle, spirits very low,
Then a knight in shining armour came, to offer us a tow.

Having put all this behind us one beautiful sunny day,
Off we went again, enjoying ourselves, once again, all OK,
Then along swam a beautiful Labrador, thought he'd cadge a ride,
So we pulled him aboard, yes you can guess, he wet everything inside.

Yet looking back now, boating is fun,
I'm not saying it suits everyone,
But boating people, to my mind,
Are tough, resilient, fun-loving and kind.

Eileen Handley

FREESTYLE

From the splash that ends the dive
To the bar when you arrive
A fish-like turn so full of grace
Then down the pool in frantic haste
The muscles crack with extra strain
The nerves they tingle with extra pain
Still you know you're in a race
You beat the water increase your pace
All you know is you must win
If you don't then why begin?

Matt Pearson

SEA-BORNE

I saw the sea rocking those see-saw waves
So gently. The ocean is the cradle,
And the infants hearken to the fable
That lulls them to sleep: and the fiction saves
Them from reality, where waves are slaves
To the tyrannical deep. Enable
The children to dream rocking horses white;
That will not disturb them with a white night.
The waves roll their eyes in dreamy surprise,
Where a supernatural story lies
Celebrating a white lie rocking still.
A tempest spells doom with an argent quill:
The waves awake, reality rages;
Fate is writing on those swelling pages.

William Edward Lewis (Junior)

SWIMMING LESSON

My sons are learning
Oh, why can't I?
I watch them swimming -
I'd rather die!
I make a promise
I'll have a try
The instructor's coming
I catch his eye.

'I'm scared of the water'
I hear myself cry
'But I need to swim
Do you think I can try?'
'I see no problem,
I can't see why.
You just need a float'
Came his reply.

One float, then two
Oh me, oh my!
I really think
It's easier to fly.
A third, then a fourth,
I cannot deny
They would float the *Queen Mary*
But, sadly, not I.

Sonia Griffiths

AN AWFUL MAN

I went for a dip just the other day,
I often go there, it's down by my way,
As I got undressed and put on my cossie,
I tried not to care about the size of my body.

Lying in the water I felt as light as a feather,
Until I got jumped on, by a big fat feller!
I sank to the bottom just like a stone,
And emerged looking like a wrinkled old gnome!

'Ha ha!' laughed the man, 'you're really the pits,
Your cossie's come down, you're showing your bits.'
Just to show off he dived in the pool,
Leaving me standing, and feeling a fool.

After swimming around I bumped into a body,
I thought it was 'Jaws' but it was a man like Doddy!
After checking my cossie I stepped out of the water,
Only to be greeted by that awful man's laughter!

Just then, two Venus-type girls came sashaying by,
The awful man smiled and gave them the eye,
I looked at their figures and silky blond hair,
And thought, Oh why can't I be standing there?

But things have a way of paying men back,
Of blocking out the sun and making things black,
The man posed elegantly to dive like a toff,
And hitting the water his trunks got pulled off!

The girls and I just curled up with laughter,
As he swam for his trunks and looked even dafter,
With my head held high and filled full of glory,
I left the pool and that's the end of my story.

Debbie McQuiston

TREASURE SEEKERS

A blue universe beneath the ocean
        Lagoons in tropical waters
Coral reefs, undersea caves, exotic fish,
        Vegetation of varied hue
Shining, shimmering in motion
        With a radiance of silvery light
Adding splendour to the view.

Explorers, voyagers, divers of another time
        Ventured beyond the reach of light
Through the murky depths
        Down to the ocean's floor
With pumps, airlines, lead boots
        They braved danger in the sea
Encased in helmets and canvas suits.

Now, in a technological era scuba divers zoom
        In skinlike suits with cylinders of air,
Lights to pierce the gloom
        Plunging to the ocean's depths.

Now, divers search for fortune's gain
        For pleasure or work in that vast domain
Unencumbered, free to roam
        Fathoms deep in another home

Eddying currents shifting sands
        Reveal, embedded in the ocean's floor
A galleon, a ship lost with all hands
        To sail no more

A rotting hulk disgorging bullion, chattels
        Ornaments, weapons of war
Tokens of other days' battles
        Now revealed, a scuba diver's dream.

S V Smy

SWIMMING

The Centre beckons, doors stand wide; but what a funny smell inside!
You pay your money, through the gate, then down the stairs, no need to wait.
The cubicle is very small, it's hardly four by four at all.
So off you struggle with your clothes, you bang your elbows, bruise your
                                                                    nose,
Till finally your swimsuit's on . . . oh, no, it's inside out! That's wrong!
At last you're done, with swimsuit, cap, your rubber socks, and after that,
Your goggles, ear-plugs, rubber ring . . . oh, don't forget your water wings!
Now, is that all? I think that's it, so to the disinfectant dip!
Oh, why's it always icy cold? The shiver runs right from your toes,
Up both your legs and through your spine, it really isn't very kind.
In fact, I think it is quite cruel . . . but finally, you're at the pool.
Not quite; before you're at its side a wristband you must wear with pride,
When time's up, you will face inspection, and no-one will escape detection.
To stay past your allotted time may well result in a hefty fine.
Gingerly you test the water, it feels much hotter than it oughta,
But after your last icy dip, beneath the waves you gladly slip.
A length or two is not too much, but, like a rabbit in a hutch,
You find there's very little room, as screaming kiddies past you zoom,
And when the wave machine gets rough, you soon decide you've had enough.
So, out you climb, all dripping wet, trudge through the ice-bath, shower next,
Then back into your little box, re-dress, pack up your suit and socks,
Joyfully head for the front door, but next week you'll be back for more!

Marie-Therese H Russell

HIGH ON A WAVE

It wasn't *Baywatch*, no babes, no Bourbon,
With rollers coming high off the sea,
Just me and my board, taking a chance,
In an effort to be free.

Sun, sea, and sand, is really good,
As the wind whistles past my ears,
Speeding along the adrenaline flows,
I don't have any fears.

The rollers are racing, anticipating,
Surfers, high on the waves,
One cheeky chap stands on one foot,
And 'flips', as his girlfriend raves.

My wet suit is tight, with no one in sight,
As I go racing along.
This is the life for me,
I may even burst into song.

The sea is now peaceful, and calm,
As the sun sets just like a charm,
I head home feeling so good,
My board, 'What a beauty', in wood.

Michael John Swain

FISH EYE VIEW

Watch with me a while if you will,
A creature from the depth so still
Its single eye stirs without a blink,
Watching me, shadowing my every turn.

The missing link, or whatever it be,
Is in full view of all to see.
Far from extinct, the ocean abounds
With fluorescent pink and bubbling sounds.

It stalks its prey in a fearless way,
The end has come I hear you say,
Then *flash!* It turns and goes away,
Leaving us to fight another day.

David McRonald

IN THE SWIM

At the edge I stand and take
A deep breath in, it's a wonderful
Thing to be able to swim.

Squealing children holding
Hands, splashing about in
Their little arm-bands.

Classes of children come in
With their school, confidently
Jump in and out of the pool.

Graceful ladies go swimming
By, twenty two lengths, and
With their hair still dry.

To keep fit and healthy it's the
Place to start, to tone up the
Muscles and strengthen the heart.

The freedom of swimming makes
You feel so alive jumping off
The boards to make a high dive.

With a smile for the steps I
Make a dash, it's a pity it's
Only a width I can splash.

A Bytheway

FROGMAN

No games played here; nor fun!
'The Oxygen Diver' . . .
No holiday swim in the sun.
Down below - cold, bitter,
Ice cold, eye-blind, jet-black,
Oil black - death black - so black.

Below a swaying ship's belly . . .
Rising, rolling, sinking . . .
On you?
'Is there a bomb below?'
'Make safe the bomb below!'
or - 'Put your bomb below.'

Crawl, steal, and feel at death!
No errors, no cowards, no folly
No fun.
Sea warriors fighting . . .
The Hun.

A Mac Gábann

SWIMMING LESSONS

I must be dim
To learn to swim
At fifteen years of age.
Into the water!
I feel that I oughter
Be better and so in a rage
I sink down the pool
And feel such a fool,
Like an elephant still in its cage.

I must be daft!
I need a raft
To stop me going down.
I look strange at my years
As the little old dears
And toddlers watch me drown
All thanks to the breed
Where you have to succeed
Oh, I really must look like a clown.

Alison Jacobs

OCEAN MEDITATION

It's a way back to our infancy,
Never feeling afraid or alone,
Naked by its consoling drone.
Overwhelmed by the ocean are we,
Captured by its powerful motion,
Endlessly transpiring deep emotion.
No money or potions to subdue tragedy,
Caressing the mind is its only tool,
Enveloping us with its dulcet call.

Penetrating our spirit with its dance,
Reverberated voices in our mind ease,
Eternally changing its vigour to please.
Valiant, mysterious, so full of chance,
Always a friend, and to make it complete,
It laps at the shore like a mother's heartbeat.
Limits are none for its love to enhance,
Satisfies our soul, reunites us with the womb,
      The ocean becomes our
          solace
   till
      the
    tomb.

Daniel Jones

SURFING CITY

I am a surfer, bold and free
see the people looking at me
Now you see me, now you doubt
as the waves ferociously leap about

The power I feel cannot be met
by any other sporting set
A rubber suit to keep me warm
while seeking a wave from dusk 'til dawn

This is a life, free and brave
loving the sea, and trusting to save
from any fear that I may hold
when a monster of a wave does unfold

The ocean has the power to
lift the meek 'derring do'
With your board keep in control
and the sea will respect your soul

A surfer, is he free as he sings
tied to the ocean's apron strings?
Wherever the wave is, he will be
as if it were his destiny

But to all the surfers everywhere
a prayer and a thought with you I share
always be safe and carefree
riding the waves 'til eternity

Gena K Crawford

MUM'S A REAL BEACH BUM

Whilst holidaying in Greece one year
We decided to join the fun,
And went off to a beach party
Dad us kids and Mum.

One of the adult games they played
Meant running into the sea,
And swopping over costumes
I was surprised that Mum agreed.

Mum and Dad stood in the queue
And watched the others go
I watched Mum's face grow redder
As they let their top halves show.

Her redness turned to horror
How could my Mum bare all?
She couldn't back out either
Cause she'd look a proper fool.

A relieved smile came over mother's face
As she discussed the plan she had,
Just then the ref's whistle blew
It's your turn Mum and Dad.

Dad promptly took off his shirt
Mum untied her costume string.
Dad helped Mum put on his top
And no-one saw a thing.

So pleased no-one had seen her top
Guess what Mum then done,
She didn't go deep enough into the sea
And showed the whole beach her *bum*.

Kim Bettley

A GENTLE FORM OF SPORT

I joined the over-40's swimming
club for a gentle form of sport,
no children jumping on me,
no arrogant swimmers I thought.

I jumped into an empty pool
this is more like it I said.
No youths splashing and diving
and shouting over my head.

More people arrived, and the
serious swimmers counted their laps.
The ladies swam in twos
so they could keep up with their little chats.

The pool was getting crowded,
the noise rose with talking and mirth.
What happened to my peaceful swim?
There's no noisier place on earth.

The ladies with their manicured nails
gouged my skin as I swim past.
The 'gentlemen' kicked me in my ribs
just to prove that they are fast.

I left the pool bruised and sore
as if I had been in battle.
I'll take my chances with
the children and youths, they don't behave like cattle.

P A Beard

WATER BABY I'M NOT!

Over the years I've learned a lot
To read or write or do sports
But to put me in a pool to swim
That's something I could never be taught.
I like to go for walks or ride my bike
But swimming I definitely do not like
Some people say 'It's good for you'
And, yes, that's really possibly true
But if you're scared of drowning
Then swimming is not for you.
I hate the waves in the water
And I definitely don't like the taste
I feel I am nearly gasping
If it only comes up to my waist
I shake and shiver with cold
Or maybe it's fright you see
But wherever there's a swimming pool
You definitely won't find me
I'll watch the people go diving and swim so happily
I would rather watch by the poolside, because
That's where I would rather be.

Elaine Lochè

SUMMER DAYS BY THE RIVER

I sit down on the bank and I dip my feet,
it's the middle of July and such a blazing heat,
I need to feel cool water on my skin,
so I'm messing about on the river until the sun goes in.

I'm just relaxing dozing off to sleep,
but these flies are distracting me,
but still I'm so happy, there's nothing that can beat,
messing about on the river in the summer heat.

Claire Young

HIGH DIVE

High at the top of the board,
A crowd around my ears ringing:
I breathe my concentrated breath
And see myself springing

Up, up into seamless air,
Flying on the cheers below;
Arching, tumbling and twisting
Into the deep blue window

Of chlorine and light still as glass,
The smooth, pool liquid lies,
I hit the water sleekly
The crowd's noise quickly dies.

Down, down I plunge,
Downward with a breath that burns
Then up, up to the rippling top
Where opaque light returns.

I hear now hushed expectation,
Stillness has the power to spellbind,
Then I somersault into the twisting dive,
That I have just seen in my mind.

Katie Hart

CALLING ALL WATER BABIES - SPORTY THOUGHTS!

If you can smell the chlorine
of that lovely swimming pool,
it's probably calling you
saying jump in and keep cool.

Maybe you prefer the Jet-ski
with the throttle on full speed
when the wind hits your face
it's certainly what you need.

The surfboard hits the waves
like a raindrop hits the ground
it's then you have a hobby
of which no-one else has found.

Traceyanne Chafer

AQUA SUMMER

The water looked so lovely
Shimmering in the sun,
It seemed to be the perfect place
To stop and have some fun.

I took the ball out from the car
And filled it full or air,
While Bertie found the nicest spot
To place his old deck-chair.

We changed into our swimming suits
And jumped into the water.
Auntie Cissy tripped and fell
But Uncle Albert caught her.

The ball went whizzing through the air
Back and forth with vigour.
Ethel gave it such a whack
And hit the poor old Vicar.

Water ball has now been banned,
But the Vicar's still not happy,
Next week we're off to Windermere
To try out water hockey.

Lynda Devereux

BIG TOE DAY

The local pool is the place to be
In summer, winter, autumn, spring
It's all inside, indoors you see
Whoops - my swimsuit's tight - ping!

It's the 'Gentle Swim' session
For those ailing or unsteady
Big toe in first - ooh, it's freezing
It's shiver me timbers, very heady

Splat - bravely I jump in
No more big toe nonsense
Think someone said good morning
But I've only been awake three hours

Ouch - some brute just kicked my legs
Must be all accidentally
Whizzed by complete with plastic cap and goggles
Looks ready to pilot a bi-plane especially

All this effort to keep fit
Think I've had enough today
Hurray - here comes the best bit
Reward time, chocolate bar and cup of tea.

Peggy Ruth Banks

BIKINI BIMBO

Down at the pool or the beach she will come,
That wiggling wonder with her tight little bum,
Her even bronzed body and
Sticking out chest,
The kind you would die for, wouldn't droop in a vest,
Her hair so shiny, which looks soft as silk,
She flashes a smile with teeth white as milk,
And don't the men stare and try to look tough,
As she walks round the pool just strutting her stuff,
Now girls - I know that feeling to
Commit the ultimate sin,
Don't you wish that when she passed
You could just push her in!

Sherrlee Blythin

JUST AIN'T FOR ME

Take to the water they say
But it don't take to me

And that goes for work and play
Be it simple ditch river or open sea

Some for the privilege good money will pay
But somehow all this just ain't for me

Some love it so much that by it they live and stay
Mind I admit it's good for making coffee and tea.

Clive Cornwall

THE WINDSURFER

He had to have a go he really did,
It looked so easy even for a kid.
So off he goes board in hand,
Running across the red-hot sand.

Into the water 'Macho Man'
Climb aboard if you can.
Who's that cursing out to sea?
'Oh my God' he's not with me.

Keeps falling off but won't give in,
Throbbing toes and bleeding skin.
One last time before dinner,
Just you watch I'll be a winner.

'Oh he's done it' off he goes,
Where he's going no one knows.
Two hours later not a sign,
Where is that 'Macho Man' of mine?

L B Yates

THE DIVE

I look up at the board high in the sky,
I want to go up there but I don't know why.

When I get to the top my heart starts to pound,
I don't want to look down so I look around

I see some people who've already taken a dive,
One thing reassures me they're still alive

Then I walk to the front of the ledge,
I close my eyes and step off the edge

Now I've done it I feel plucky,
You want me to go again, you should be so lucky.

Mark Tettenborn (9)

BEAUTY BENEATH THE SEA

While swimming in a sea of blue
In the Dominican republic I'll relate to you
All around a wonderland
Has oysters got pearls in their precious shells
Fish in colours so very bright
Wonderful and impressive sight
Intricate coral beautiful too
A sea garden unbelievably true
Slowly on the ocean bed
A creature lifts its lazy head
Crabs they scuttle quick as can be
And blend into the scenery
The seaweed gently floats about
Luxuriant green there is no doubt
Under the sea it is a pleasure
Could stay all day exploring to do
Magic moments for to treasure
A full tank for good measure
Underneath the sea of blue.

Sheila MacDonald

UNDER THE WAVES

No noise to disturb the tranquil beauty,
Only the reassuring sound of escaping air.
Lunar movements in an aquatic atmosphere.
A place of natural beauty and intrigue,
A place of solitude and escapism.
We'll dive as one and enjoy together the
      beauty under the waves.

Melanie Unsworth

WATER WONDERFUL WORLD

Down on the Solent
In Southsea's fine air
Me and my girlfriend
My maiden so fair
We hired a rowing boat
She looked bemused
She stared at my rowlocks
She looked quite confused
And to think, in a while
She'll have handfuls of sores
'Positioned' her right
As I gave her the oars
She weren't up to scratch
I proceeded to blast her
'I'm tryin' to water ski
Row a bit faster!'
Another good time
Was with me and my mate
We went to the baths
Met a bloke who we hate
This bloke cannot swim good
In fact he's quite thick
His water-wings burst
So I threw him a brick
He sank like a seal
On its way for some kelp
Then he floated back up
Shoutin' 'Help, someone help
I can't swim,' he pleaded
So I gave him a roastin'
'I can't play the piano
But I don't go round boastin'!'

K A Travis

BEACH BLUES

The sea is like glass
the skies turn to grey
the things I don't ask
the thing's you don't say
the wind doesn't blow through my hair
the water turns so cold
I'm crying like a baby
when the story unfolds

The nights draw in closer
the clouds move so slow
I feel I don't know you
I feel I must go
the summer is a lifetime away
the clouds move so slow
I always have the wrong thing to say
I make you feel so cold

The harbour is so empty
the boats sleep on the dry
the letters you sent me
the sunset sky
the waves don't crash on the shore
the gulls do not fly
I think I can't take anymore
then you're back in my life.

James E B Smith

WHY CAN'T I SWIM

Why can't I swim
Like the ones in the pool
I come here quite often
And I've tried to improve
But so far my efforts
Have gone with the breeze
Cause I'm panting, and spluttering
Like a whale all at sea
Can't go out of my depth
Cause I'd panic and then
Trying to reach bottom
I would sink and what then
Now look at that smarty pants
Looking at me
She's been up and down the pool
And still looks at ease
But why should I worry
I bet she can't cook
Well it makes me feel better
While I stand on one foot

Jeanette Gaffney

SWIMMING

Wet towels, wet hair, wet floor
Wet everywhere, where are we,
Why at the swimming pool.
Strange shapes, coloured caps,
Lovely legs flash by doing the
Crawl and the butterfly.
Simply divine this hobby of mine
Can't wait till next week it will be
Sublime doing the backstroke a
Favourite of mine.

Lots of people gossip and chat
Around the edge, making plans
To shop, have lunch or maybe
Go to a concert at the Cathedral
It's time to go our separate ways
Goodbye, adieu, we'll meet again
Soon, very soon.

Have a lovely day!

Margery Richards

MESSING ABOUT ON THE RIVER

A boat on the river is so much fun.
Enjoyment and pleasure for everyone.
Big boats, small boats
Anything that floats.
You stand at the wheel,
Captain's hat on head.
You need nerves of steel,
your face very red,
When you enter a lock for the very first time,
and bump into the side, and lose hold of the line.
You rock and you roll
in a slimy green hole.
When big black gates open and out you can go.
Once more into sunshine,
but this time go slow.
So the wash from your craft
doesn't do anything daft.
Enjoy the rivers flow,
respect and revere,
the river so bright, crystal clean and clear.
So everyone else can enjoy it as well,
when they safely arrive home
their story to tell.

B Gates

THE KING POOL OF THE RIVER OF MILK

Cooling and shimmering the waters call with its rugged rocks
and water falls,
the children play excitedly, screamed out with passion,
happiness and glee
so inviting . . . so tantalising . . . its power I knew revitalising

My son beckoned to join in the fun, I feasted on his pleasure
then up to the sun
Its heat bore down tingling my skin
its burning intensified the longing within

The yearning heightened, I became less frightened
less afraid of the beasties and cold
and so with an intake of breath and an upsurge of will
I submerged my feet . . . my shins . . . until . . .

A slip, a slide, under the water did ungracefully glide
surfacing to embarrassment and laughter
I tried to regain what little pride remained
feeling more than a litter dafter . . . err

But fate, it was decided that day
I was not to have it my own way
and whilst for my sandals my husband searched
I crept back to the banking and on it perched.

Kathleen Schmidt

BE SAFE

Before you ever start to dive
It is important that you survive
There are lots of things for you to check.
Before you go heading for a wreck
Give that belt an extra pull
Then make sure the tanks are full
If the pressure is too low.
Don't take a chance you don't go.

Try to forget about the bill
Get yourself a refill
There are lots of things to take with you
So lots of more checks to get through
Only when all your buddy checks are done
Then go diving and have some fun.
Sorry to be a pain in the rear
But we want you safe and all back here.
This is where my poem ends
So go safe and be lucky all my diving friends.

Philip E Cox

WATER

Water in your whiskey, water in your gin,
The first is perfect culture, the second mortal sin.
A single malt with ice cubes, water in your beer,
Tolerating either is infra-dig, I hear.
Water round our beaches in which we love to play,
Is full of muck and sewage, and worsens by the day.
The water in our rivers should flow both sweet and clear,
But most are open sewers, or so it would appear.
Water in your rain butt, water on your lawn,
Both are what is needed, is our hope forlorn?
Rain is where it comes from, it hasn't rained for weeks,
Yet all the main suppliers, waste lots because of leaks.
'Share your bath' they tell us, but of this I'm not so sure,
I couldn't share with neighbours, *except for her next door*
We mustn't use our hosepipes for garden or the car,
These silly bans were issued much too late by far.
For now it's started raining as hard as e'er I've seen,
The weather's causing flooding of reservoir and stream
The bans are still enforced though, stupidity so crass,
The reason we're aware of, the law is such an ass.

'Bunny' Newman

THE SEA THE SEA

The good Lord walked on water
Now, that was good man, that was great;
Now me, I have a lovely daughter
Who dives into the deepest water
And trusts far more than me
In fate.

Quite honestly,
She just can't have enough
Of the bloomin' stuff,
Emergin' out, all smooth an' wet,
I have to smile at her
And yet . . .

Don't laugh -
I like to take a bath
Now and again
As most men
Do.
Well, come to that,
I have to, once a week,
Just to take a peek
At what God made us for,
To ruminate
And contemplate
Our navels,
Nothing more,
In water not too deep,
But just enough to float in
And sail our little boats in.

The sea, the sea
Is not for me.

Hal Cheetham

COME TO THE POOL

Come to the pool from nine to ten,
Over fifty ladies, gosh - no men.
Please be brave this pool is cool,
This ageing game is very cruel.

Who's that diving, down deep end,
It's Anne Marie an old school friend.
What is she wearing on her head!
A floral shower cap blue and red.

I think I'll join her for a chat,
And comment on her fancy hat.
She says 'You know it is my perm,
I hope to make it last one term.'

Then she dives and flops about,
Sometimes whale and sometimes trout.
I say 'look out see my new stroke,'
She laughs and says 'it's one big joke.'

And now five ladies in a ring,
Swim up and down the pool - big thing.
The gossips hot 'she - she - she - he,'
They slowly swim and float past me.

I stretch my hand to get a'float,
The chlorine trickles down my throat.
I'm feeling cold I've had enough,
This swimming lark is really tough.

The pool attendants smile and grin,
They look so fit and very thin,
One blows his whistle, wipes his brow,
Over fifty ladies, 'Get out now.'

Catherine Long

BELOW THE SURFACE

We're all kitted up and ready to go,
To find secret treasures of the sea down below
The beauty a diver may catch a glimpse of,
Could keep him spellbound, enchanted smitten, in love!

The tropical sea water laps on my face,
Then descending, I see fishes gliding with grace.
Their colours as abundant as their shapes and their size,
Trigger fish, troupers, reef sharks - what a prize!

The silvery glints of Barracudas all around,
Quite spectacular, infrequent, oh and the sound.
The moray eels watching, vicious teeth just ajar,
Remind us of ocean's dangers. Don't touch that star!

A shipwreck houses creatures of interest for all,
It's now a silent shadow, where men once would call.
Unfortunate fishermen, their nets left behind,
Are now feeding stations for fishes. How very kind!

The warm water helps corals to abundantly grow,
They're colourful during the day but at night they do glow.
Bright fluorescence flicker in the dark sea abyss,
On land is there anything as beautiful as this?

Manta rays silently appear out of the deep,
These prehistoric creatures glide past - quick take a peep.
There's landing crafts rusting from during World War Two,
Each time you go diving you see something new.

What BSAC has taught stands all in good stead,
With pool training and lectures, - everything's fresh in your head.
The sea really is a marvellous place,
Let's protect it and respect it, for our great grandchildren's race!

Ruth L Ironside

SURF VERSUS ME

'I would love to go,' I muttered to the phone I clutched in bed,
still asleep, I again said 'yes' and promptly forget what I had said

As the doorbell rang twice, I grabbed my robe from the floor,
fell over the cat and on the third ring, managed to grab the door

There stood Alex smiling, 'um hello', was all that I could say,
as I remembered with horror, I had agreed to go surfing today.

'I am glad you agreed' said Alex, 'I thought it was a good idea,'
and soon we were carrying surfboards along a windy pier.

The water was not as cold as it looked, but the surf was high,
just right, I was told, 'yes', I'm looking forward to surfing I lied.

'Ride the wave,' Alex said, but the board just turned upside down,
as I grabbed from below he shouted, 'ride it the other way round'

I glared at the fibre glass thing and I swear it grinned at me,
as I climbed aboard once more, it reared and flung me in the sea

I tried again and again, but even lying down, I still fell off,
I saw Alex smirking, I suspect because I couldn't stay aloft

I am sure it was amusing, purple bikini versus surf and sea,
next time I would bring string and tie the board to me!

At last the evening came, thank you I said then turned to go,
but too late I saw that surfboard I tripped and broke a toe

So it had won the day for now but I'd be back again I swore,
to beat that bit of fibre glass, as I hobbled to the shore.

Jil Bramhall

THE FANATIC

      Nonchalant
he launches his shark-finned craft
becomes part of it,
catches the wind.
Limbs straining, torso bronzed as a
tomb-frieze warrior's, he is sea-born,
becomes a sea creature, part man,
part bird, part fish.

Navigator, cormorant, dolphin,
he manipulates waves, thrills to
wind, spray, speed, the struggle.
No longer of this world -
a Hermes, a Puck, an Ariel,
the elements are his life, his breath,
mind and muscle devoted bond-slaves.

He resists invisible bull-dozers;
the board's prow lifts, everything
blurs, stings, whips; he ricochets
from wave-crest to wave-crest,
now almost air-borne, now
sweeping down spume-flecked slopes,
now free-falling; he concedes
this is addictive, hallucinogenic,
revels in a dream state.

Robert Lumsden

SURFING

I wrestle with the wrestling tide;
Riding the breakers high
Daring the power of the waves;
And like a bird I fly.

Lost in a world of sea and spray;
Tossed by the restless sea
Keeping aboard my flimsy craft
While the wild waves surge free.

The spray is flung into my face
It's salty tang I taste,
And hear the roar of the roaring waves
As on the shore they break.

A roller towers overhead
With tons of water poised
To crash upon me as I ride
And breaks with thunderous noise

In a wild surging water world
I struggle to regain
My balance, fragile though it be
And on my board remain.

Sometimes I win, and taste the thrill
Of racing to the shore
Carried impetuously along
Riding a surging bore;

And sometimes lose, though it's no shame
For powerful is the sea
If I but win sometimes, then it
Is good enough for me.

Sybil Sibthorpe

BOBBING ABOUT IN THE RIVER!

Oh yes! I was in that canoe,
in this river as wide as a sea,
in weather that's driven the ducks back to bed
and on waves I'd been warned, 'disagree'

The Instructor, he'd ordered a roll -
even showed us the way it was done,
but despite me discomfort, it could have been worse -
like what might be below when I'd spun.
So I paddled about at the back,
pretending, 'I'll do it with ease!'
And when they'd gone under, I wetted me hair,
then pretended again, 'what a breeze!'

But that man, he had eyes like a hawk
and he spotted me skiving his wish
so then I'd to do it, in front of the class -
With the skill of a somersault fish.
Well, I took in a very deep breath,
held the oar in me hand, like he'd said
and prayed to Almighty, 'I'll do it this time!'
As the water surrounded me head.

Oh yes! I was in that canoe,
it's heading right now for dry land.
The Instructor? He's shouting, but ah, never mind.
'Sir, I've still got the oar in me hand!'

Angela Rogerson

TRY A SNORKEL OR TWO!

Hot sunny skies, a sea of clear blue,
A place on the beach just made for two,
The mountains of Jordan on one side. Eilat,
And the Red Sea between in the bit that is flat.

What more could we want to see or to do,
You ask, but it's nice to try something new
So we gathered a snorkel and mask, coloured pink,
And timidly stood at the sea, on the brink.

It's hard to find words with snorkel in mouth
A nod and advance with courage, go south,
Head under, a splutter, oh why does the sea
Go down through the tube, and try to drown me!

For those on the shore, the scene is a laugh
With bottoms seen cruising with plenty ballast,
Water fountains are frequent in seas azure blue
And the snorkeller is seen, turning red, white, the hue!

But after some practice, what fun can be had
When you master the skill, silent worlds make you glad,
The glorious corals and fishes galore
Excite nearly everyone, can't wait for more.

The underworld's silent, brilliant colour and hue.
Large fish and small, star fish bright blue,
Shells fluted and flat, sea urchins and eels
What a wonderful world under water reveals.

I bet you can't wait to go there again
To that hot, sunny clime with no sign of rain,
Eilat is a paradise, water babes hear!
For snorkellers and divers, we'll join you next year!

Elizabeth M Sudder

WATERSPRITE

Boy on a dolphin,
Happy and free,
Bouncing about on the deep blue sea,
Boy on a dolphin,
Having such fun,
Spending your life 'neath the golden sun,
Boy on a dolphin,
Hasn't a care,
Riding the waves in the clear fresh air,
Boy on a dolphin,
What would I give,
If ever and aye like you I could live.

Dorothy Neil

MAYBE

Far from the dire and deep cold sea
Dig me my hole and leave me be;
All my long life I never could see
How others could find it a thrill,
To dote on and dive in it,
Float on and thrive on it,
Go out and get under it
To pillage and plunder it,
Or write a book on it
Or even look on it
Seems fishy to me;
But push out the boat a bit
I might even vote for it;
Well maybe . . .
Let's see!

L R Frost

PRIDE COMES BEFORE A PLUNGE

When I was twelve I made up my mind
It was time I learned to swim.
My brother was his class champion,
And I longed to be like him.

Trouble was I hadn't a swim-suit,
So it seemed my luck was out,
'Til my aunt said that I could have one of hers -
'You're quite big, it'll fit you no doubt.'

Feeling every inch the lady,
I gingerly stepped in the pool,
Little guessing what was in store for me -
My swim-suit was made of wool!

I made my way to the deep end.
I thought I was doing fine,
Completely oblivious to what was going on
Beneath the water line.

The deeper I waded the more my suit sagged,
'Till I realised with shock
That by now it was down to my ankles.
You'd have thought I was wearing a frock!

Swathed in yards of sopping wet wool -
Every single movement a task -
How did I manage to vacate that pool?
Please, do me a favour - don't ask!

Dorothy White

GOING DOWN

Wetsuit on, zips secure
Mask and snorkel firmly on face
Final check on air supply
Roll over the edge to the place

The place that is silent,
Calm and serene
Fans dance to the gentle current
Neptune's grass poke up in between.

Ten metres, twenty metres,
Check on air supply.
This'll do, I'll wait a while,
Perch on a reef to see what passes by

An eagle ray, a moray eel
An octopus trying to hide
Damsel fish bedecked in blue
Flashing far and wide.

A buzz of activity!
All fish suddenly move
Tuna! Tuna!
Predators on the loose.

The gauge is showing 100
The clock is ticking too
Time to go, back to the bustle
Of life in the human zoo.

I'll have to wait till next time
To go down to that place
To float weightless, dance around
To swim with the fish in a state of grace.

Jayne Hilary Lowry

GEARED UP

On goes the suit,
The boots and the gloves,
Encased now in rubber,
It's almost perverse!
Stab jacket and tank,
Weight belt and more
And I'm supposed to swim!
Is that right?
Are you sure?

With all this strapped on,
I must weigh a ton!
And I was informed,
That diving was fun
All of those claims
Were they just talk?
How can I swim?
I can't even walk!

With fins on my feet,
And tank on my back
Out of the water
Grace I certainly lack.
The water takes the weight, you'll see
Or so they keep on telling me
Till then, I suppose, I'll wait, I'll fret
You see this is one diver
Yet to get wet

L Medcalf

DADDY'S GONE OUT DIVING

Daddy's gone out diving,
For a short holiday.
He'll see lots of wildlife,
If he gets his way.

Daddy's gone out diving
For a couple of days.
Soon he'll take his boat out,
To ride along the waves.

Daddy's gone out diving,
For a long weekend.
I know that he will miss me,
So postcards he will send.

Daddy's gone out diving,
For an exciting break
I know that he'll be back,
But how long will he take!

Daddy's gone out diving,
For a week or two.
But now he's back I'm really glad,
For we're going to the zoo.

Michelle Devine (10)

ORCA-ENVY

Black and white
>round of face
Lords of speed
>and sinister grace
Five foot fin
>that spans the earth
Pity their warm womb
>cold sea birth
They came with us
>from out of the slime
Walked with us through aeons of time
When we stood up
>they went to swim
Our fingers spread theirs formed a fin

So must we upon the land
>Touch the sea with poisoned hand
Destroy the oceans' living waters
>and boil the sea-king's
soft skinned daughters

Marne Eric Watts

EMBARRASSING MOMENT

To swimming I went at Pimlico Square -
At work I changed clothes before I got there.
Then I stood at the edge; my outer clothes doffed
I looked down - oh dear,
>my underwear's not off!

Dawn Stangi

THE GALLEON

It was cold and wet
When I first met Sally
She was looking rather old
her smile was faded
and her lips no longer red
the salt had taken its
toll on Sally.
She led them all to sea,
beauty and grace, accompanied
her every sailing
Turning heads in every port
the sailors wished she were real.
Then came the day,
She carried a priceless treasure
They didn't look at Sally
as they filled her body with fire.
She sank like a stone
and came to rest right here
Where today I meet her face to face,
no longer leading fleet
just resting her sole
and still turning heads

Wayne Ford

NEVER TOO LATE TO LEARN

For years I've had a secret wish, I just wanted one small thing.
But money always being tight, I never learnt to swim.
Kids grown up and off my hands, why not have a go.
But thyroid trouble made me fat, out of breath and slow.
Medication did the trick, I soon became much thinner.
In a swimsuit I looked good, come on girl you're a winner.
Look close into the mirror, you know it won't tell lies.
Oh God! what can I do, just look at my poor thighs.
Pride comes before a fall they say, I really am a sap.
The purple veins make my poor legs, look like an old roadmap
Calm down in just an hour or two, laid on a good sunbed
You'll change from being greyish white, to chocolate brown instead
I'm ready now to take the plunge all tanned and looking trimmer
Nothing else stands in my way I'll soon become a swimmer
The learners class, eight-thirty start, I've waited here since eight
Making sure I'd be on time, no way would I be late.
This lesson is for oldies, so I'm not out of place
I hope I'll soon be gliding, through the water with some grace
After a few lessons, I'm really in the swim.
So now I'd like so spend some time on another whim.
What shall I do with my free time, hang on now that's a thought
Perhaps with my new energy, I'll become an *Astronaught*
But looking at my spelling of a word like this
I think I'll take an English course and give outerspace a miss.

J Walters

FARNE ISLAND DIVE

We travelled slowly huddled down
to miss the freezing spray.
Wondered if the coxswain knew
for certain where the islands lay

We travelled slowly looking aft
to keep the land in view.
Wondered if the coxswain felt
the fear that we all knew

We travelled slowing holding tight
to thoughts of fireside dives.
Wondered if the coxswain's mind
could stray from points and tides

We travelled in a world of white
and blue and darker grey.
Wondered if the coxswain'd noticed
the land had slipped away

We travelled in a world of noise
tight lipped to show no nerve.
Wondered if the coxswain's brain
had comprehended the sound of surf

We dropped the anchor prepared to dive
by a rock, putrid, massive, hard.
Wondered if the coxswain's plan
was lodged with the local coastguard.

We pulled each other into the boat
reluctantly from a dead calm sea.
Wondered if the coxswain'd planned
a dive for next Sunday

C Smith

UNTITLED

This is the story of Myrtle Snell,
Who into Sale Marina fell.
Whose mum had said 'You never oughta,
Go too near the deep dark water.'

To the bottom she did hurtle,
Ears a pounding (poor old Myrtle),
She landed on Marina bed,
Into the arms of diver Fred.

Into action Fred then sprung,
As Myrtle tightly to him clung.
He guided her up to the top,
And lo, her ears began to pop.

Myrtle went and learned to swim,
Then joined a dive club on a whim.
Who should she meet there? Fred you know,
Before too long he was her beau.

Said Myrtle 'Did you ever think,
That when I fell into the drink,
A wife you'd find in your watery lair,
Someone to cook, and share your air?'

Said Fred 'With me you fell in love,
What turned you on my turtle dove?'
Said Myrtle 'Twas your kiss of life
That made me want to be your wife . . .

I liked it . . . !'

Pat Cunliffe

THE BEAUTY OF THE SEA

The sea is a beautiful, underwater, land
With fish, pretty flowers and the bright yellow sand,
Starfish, crabs, which will pinch your toes!
A swordfish with a very sharp nose!
Dolphins, turtles , sharks and seals
A porpoise and a conger eel.

>Lots of exploring for you and me,
>That's, the beauty of the sea!

Peering through the big, grey, rocks,
I had myself a great big shock!
A family of fishes, big and small
Amongst the seaweed so very tall!

They looked so pretty, coloured and bright
It looked such a beautiful, wonderful sight!
Then I put the rock back, where it was found,
And there was nothing but silence all around.

I swam much further, ever so deep,
Amongst the pretty, coral reefs.
Some were red, some were green,
The most prettiest, prettiest ever seen!

>Lots of exploring for you and me
>That's the beauty of the sea!

Kirsty MacDougall (11)

EARLY MORNING DIVE

The storm winds howled and timbers creaked,
Strange noises through the night,
We woke to grey and o'ercast skies,
Then sun - oh happy sight!

The dhoni took us out to sea,
Maayafushi Tilla dive,
Rahman he led us to the sharks,
They numbered more than five.

We crouched beneath the overhang,
Sharks circled slowly by,
Large grey with vicious grinning mouth
And glittering black steel eye.

The smaller white tips ventured near,
And cameras flashed and clicked,
A twenty minute cabaret show,
Best coral seats hand picked.

We did not threaten these fine fish,
So soon they swam away,
We surfaced, all elated with
The first dive of the day.

Valerie Sheldon

THE REEF

Look above
The boat hangs in the blue,
dark bottomed
Look away

I watch tiny fish hide in a coral flower,
peeping out as a shadow passes
then one by one resume their dance.

Look above
The hull points to the deep,
between us, feel the water's weight.
Look away

I watch a turtle sleeping on a ledge,
shell dappled in a shaft of light.
Do not breathe, do not disturb its trust.

Look above
A window opens on the world,
clouds seem to float beneath the waves
Look away

I watch with never ending awe,
a million things as yet unseen.
Regret the wasted surface hours.

Look below
Rising nearer to the sun
mask down, the reef now indistinct
keeps pulling, never letting go,
Look above

Deborah Edge

THE WATERS OF AVALON

The clinking of a bell-buoy drifts across a gentle swell
And the greenlight blinking on the harbour wall, atests
To celestial navigators surfing in on the dusk, that all is well.
Nature's most violent elements are at rest.
No mixing of two worlds into a frothy hell,
Pounded against the rocky shoreline to the west.

Inside this body, behind these eyes, I look on
At a tranquil scene in the world of air and light,
But my soul slips beneath the waters of Avalon
And glides through its dark and silky-silent night,
One of a myriad of creatures moving, following in abandon,
A thin strand of consciousness to an unknown plight.

Spirit has inhabited both these worlds, alike.
'Here are your waters and your watering place.'
It penetrates every chink, except lungs and eyes,
To reach the skin, cool against the face.
A counterbalancing of forces, here gravity can be denied,
Tilting the scales of reality to a transcendent grace.

Moving in three dimensional space with the sea bass,
Amongst the kelp fronds' lattice-green rafts,
With the flame-orange Garibaldis and sheepshead wrasse,
A million tiny fish glittering and darting in sunlit shafts.
Crossing a membrane between water and depth-compressed gas,
Trickling, growing, ascending like shattered, silver-glass shards.

My soul again breaks into the world of air
And follows shafts of light into my shore-bound eyes.
Into the recesses of a world of quiet despair,
Inhabited by ghosts and strangled cries,
Placated by a journey to a world of calm repair,
A transcendent equilibrium that reason defies.

Richard J Heads

DON'T STOP BREATHING

What a silly comment, or so I thought
When a mask, snorkel and lessons I excitedly bought.
As if I'd stop, it's natural to inhale.
But I must admit, the words made me turn pale.
      Although I kept on breathing.

I listened to lectures, calculated times from a table.
Found reassurance, for in Maths I'm quite able,
But was I physically fit enough at forty-odd
To try to exist in the domain of the cod?
      While still breathing.

I took off my mask, replaced it with care
Though it took some time to free all my hair.
Removed my weights, replaced them again
Did the same with my jacket, while I counted to ten.
      Always breathing.

Buoyancy skills needed practice and more
As I rose and fell on the ocean floor.
But at last came the time when I felt at ease
And swam quite far without knocking my knees.
      Placidly breathing.

Then came the ascent without any air
To say I was frightened is not really fair.
The instructor had shown how straight forward it was
And he was right to have confidence, you see, because
      I'm still breathing.

Kerry Lee

SUNKEN DREAMS

Descending down to discover the deep
Thoughts of treasure and trophies to keep
Darker, deeper, darker, down,
Nothing to see just murky brown.

Then suddenly joyfully out of the gloom
The familiar shape of a wreck will loom.
It's hard to suppress an excited grin.
But make it too wide and water comes in.

Now sort out your kit, all in its place
Continue the dive at leisurely pace
Over plates of rusting, twisted metal you pass.
Home to the cod and pollock and wrasse.

Silently moving stealthily through
Suspended and weightless in awe of the view.
The wreck is so peaceful she is at rest.
Her secrets she's holding close to her chest.

Holes in her structure gaping wide.
The darkness beckoning you inside.
You reach for your torch, turn on the beam
The cavern lights up revealing a dream.

Gold coins and jewels a chest of doubloons
Trinkets and diamonds the size of balloons
Heart beating, eyes popping, can it be true?
Alright! I know! But you can dream can't you?

You look at your gauge, it's time to go up.
Your time underwater is never enough.
The wreck gets smaller as you float away,
Already planning to return next day.

Mick Devine

IN TOO DEEP

Like men in space, all suits, no skin
Am I to face foe or kin?
The shimmering blue, the shafts of light
every colour and hue, my senses fight

The creatureless houses, the talcum sand
what feelings it arouses as it touches my hand
bubbles to the surface like champagne corked
penetrating the abyss, should we abort?

The seabed long, the dragging tide
forces so strong, too late to hide
ebony consumes me, silt swirls around
I strain to see treasures I've found

The light is dim, cold grabs hold
why did we begin to be so bold?
Fish eyes staring, the timid hide
check our bearing, stay by my side

We start to rise, warmth greets flesh
leaving the prize, now terrestrial mess
breathing the air, sky in view
consciously aware our time is through.

Suzy Walsh

DIVE

Falling, sliding, between sheets of water.
Silky smooth, cool, dark, inviting
enclosing, comforting,
serene.
This world apart,
intruders, we dip into lives,
theirs not ours.
Theirs is
calm, now woken, broken.
Spent air, rising spirals,
sparkling jewels of life.
Silent.
Surrounding, dropping, sinking,
spying, prying, flying.
Suspended in their world.
Deeper yet, and down,
rusting, trusting wreckage, sewage.
Hunting, seeking, poking, searching, intruding.
Our wreck, our message.
Our legacy.
Not theirs.
Rising, leaving, rejected, elated.
Time spent, air too.
Closing behind, hiding, living.
Their world, our solution.
Their problem.
Now ours.

Keith Pritchett

DIVING FREE

We search for the knowledge that comes from the sea,
The fish and the plants, they all fascinate me,
We dive to the wrecks on the seabed below,
To discover the things that we do not yet know.

No longer we wait for the depths they do call,
We push off our boat from the old harbour wall,
Make fast our anchor and then start our dive,
Leave the surface behind us, we feel so alive.

The wonders we see give us thrills of elation,
Of fish and small creatures from all of creation,
So close I could touch them, unconcerned about me,
There at the bottom's what I've come to see.

The wreck of a ship long forgotten by most,
Concealed by the sea off this bleak Cornish Coast,
Old wooden timbers encrusted with barnacles,
Alive now with sea life and weed with long tendrils.

The ebb and the flow of the tide take their toll,
For pieces lie scattered which once made the whole
My hands touch the timbers and I feel from her vibes,
Those who had sailed her and gave her their lives.

Beneath her old bow are rocks that have torn,
A great jagged hole and to this we are drawn,
Small pieces of metal perhaps they're quite old,
Something to treasure when our stories be told.

My pressure gauge tells me our visit must end,
So back to the surface, but must slowly ascend,
We sit on the sand, talk of wrecks and the sea
For we all feel this great longing, a need to be free.

Ann Guilder

NOTICE OF A NEW NAVIGATIONAL HAZARD IN CHANNEL

Here's a saga of the sea
Of our member, Big John B
So you divers gather round
Take note of these words, profound.

You don't need to be clairvoyant
Knowing dry suits are quite buoyant
So you equalise with lead
And swim like a fish instead.

This lead's buckled round your waist
With quick release to drop in haste
But remember it's no fun
If it snags and comes undone.

John was taken by surprise
With clawing hands and bulging eyes
He knew his, *Northfleet* dive was ended
As he rapidly ascended.

Bursting up towards the surface
Mouthing foul and obscene curses
Like an acrobatic clown
Not headfirst but *upside down!*

Sailors if to Lydd you voyage
Please take note of new wreck buoyage,
There protruding from the sea
The *Northfleet*'s marked with a victory 'V'!

The Stowting Bard

DIVE FEVER

I must go down to the sea again,
to the lonely sea and sky,
and all I ask is a high powered rib,
and a GPS to steer her by.

And the kick of the plane and the depths' song,
and the hiss of a freeflowing DV,
and the DO's shouted blunders,
and the crew's moan
throwing their guts asunder.

I must go down to the seas again,
to the call of a running tide,
to a seven knot drift
and the chopper's whump
and the mayday call, which cannot be denied.

I must go down to the wreck again,
to the call a the brass a' beckoning,
to the fizz of live shells and the -
- panicked prayer,
and the silt like a feared nightmare.

And all I ask is a 100w lamp,
to light up the be'silted porthole
and an air saw and a crowbar,
and a mantlepiece when dive's over.

Ian Geraint Jones

DEEP SEA DIVER

I'm a deep sea diver
and my favourite place to be
is swimming around in the water,
deep down, under the sea.

All sense of fear is abandoned,
all sense of time is misplaced,
I just look on and wonder
at the beauty with which I am faced.

Creatures circle around me,
almost touching my hand.
Beautiful, colourful creatures,
like you'd never imagine on land.

Everything seems to move slowly,
smoothly, calmly around.
Fish swim neatly beside me,
without even making a sound.

I'm sure that if I were able,
I'd spend hours and hours down there,
but when you're a human, you've no choice
but to come to the surface for air!

W V Ponting

FIRST NERVES

One step, what lies beneath will soon unfold,
the world below is drawing near,
Pulling me down, I take a breath,
the excitement enhanced by fear,
A rush of air, darkness, my breath I hold
I fumble around, then all becomes clear,
A beam of light, I watch as colours swim by,
the floor is moving, it's alive . . .
Vibrant corals, shoals of fish surround me,
I forget my fear.
My buddy signals, it's time to ascent,
A shadow looms, the boat is above me,
Civilisation is here . . .

C Meredith

INFORMATION

We hope you have enjoyed reading this book - and that you will continue to enjoy it in the coming years.

If you like reading and writing poetry drop us a line, or give us a call, and we'll send you a free information pack.

Write to

        Arrival Press Information
        1-2 Wainman Road
        Woodston
        Peterborough
        PE2 7BU.